CW01217078

ROCKY
The Ultimate Guide

ROCKY
The Ultimate Guide

By Edward Gross

Contents

Foreword..6

Making *Rocky*.......................................8

ROCKY

The Italian Stallion............................12

Paulie..14

Adrian..16

Apollo Creed.......................................18

Rising to the Challenge....................20

Mickey and the Gym.........................22

The Training.......................................24

The Fight...26

The Final Round................................28

ROCKY II

Gloves and Marriage.........................32

Money and Losing It........................34

Creed vs. the Stallion Chicken........36

The Vigil..38

Rocky's Back.......................................40

The Rematch......................................42

The Decider..44

ROCKY III

The Champ..48

Thunderlips!.......................................50

Clubber Lang......................................52

The Challenge....................................54

The First Fight...................................56

The Aftermath...................................58

Starting Over......................................60

Second Chance..................................62

The Favor..64

ROCKY IV

East vs. West......................................68

Ivan Drago..70

Press Conference..............................72

All-American Show......................................74

Apollo's Last Fight......................................76

West vs. East..78

Welcome to Russia......................................80

Fighting Fit..82

Ready?..84

Avenging Apollo..86

Making Peace..88

ROCKY V

Paying the Price..92

George Washington Duke..............................94

Riches to Rags..96

Mick's Place..98

Tommy Gunn..100

Training Tommy..102

Family Life..104

Heavyweight Champ..................................106

Street Fight..108

Rocky Wins..110

ROCKY BALBOA

Rocky's World..114

Family and Friends....................................116

Mason 'The Line' Dixon..............................118

Man vs. Machine......................................120

Meet the Press..122

Back In Training......................................124

Pre-Fight..126

The Last Fight..128

BEHIND THE SCENES

Rocky..132

Rocky II, III, IV, and V................................134

Rocky Balboa..136

Props..138

Glossary..140

Index..142

Acknowledgments....................................144

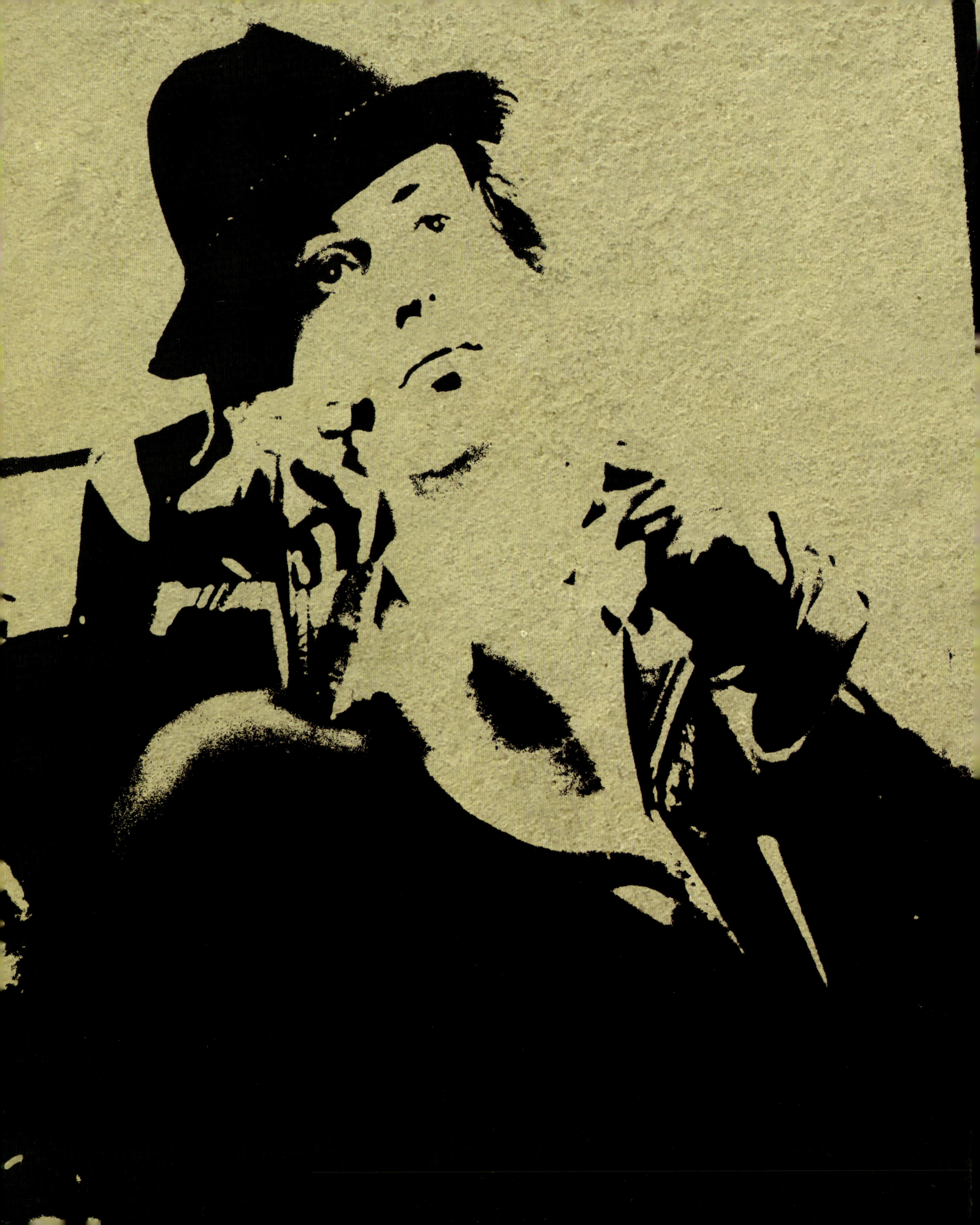

Foreword

It was near freezing I believe, both outside on the streets of Philly one bleak morning that would be the first shot of the movie *Rocky*, and inside my veins, where ice water seemed to be coursing through my limbs. I was at a crossroad in my life. I had dreamt the dream, talked the talk, and now, at 4:30 AM, was the moment when illusion would intersect with reality. Would I fail to live up to my expectations? Would *Rocky* be a journey no one could relate to or even bother to give a sidelong glance to? "I'd rather do something I love badly, than feel bad about not doin' something I love," I thought.

Maybe I wasn't alone in this. Maybe the world is bursting at the seams with the broken-hearted who have never had their chance to stand toe to toe with life and give it their best shot; the chance to go the distance; the chance to taste defeat or victory; the chance to either watch the game or be in it because in the end all that really matters is having the opportunity to play. Opening the door and feeling that arctic blast assault my body, I suddenly felt very warm.

Sylvester Stallone

Making Rocky

IT WAS SYLVESTER STALLONE'S screenplay, in particular its ending, that first attracted producers Robert Chartoff and Irwin Winkler to *Rocky*. That ending, with the hero triumphing in a quite unexpected way, hinted at something very different from the convential sports movie. "From my point of view, the appeal was the fact that Rocky lost the fight," says Chartoff. "That was the key element for me and after I finished the script, I immediately said, 'This is a movie that I want to make.' It was so off the track from everything else that one reads. The hero actually loses and is still a hero and still has good values and he had his own internal battle that he had fought. I liked that idea a lot." A good part of that internal battle came from Stallone himself. "There are certain parallels between Rocky and me," he admits. "Rocky had drive and intelligence and the talent to be a fighter, but nobody noticed him. The second ingredient had to be me, my particular story, my inability to be recognized. I felt Rocky to be the perfect vehicle for that kind of sensibility. So I took my story and injected it into the body of Rocky Balboa, because no one, I felt, would be interested in listening to or watching or reading a story about a down-and-out struggling actor/writer."

THE IDEA

The initial idea for the story that was to become *Rocky* was born out of the struggle its creator was himself experiencing as a young writer/actor. As the film celebrated its 30th anniversary in 2006, Sylvester Stallone reflected on the concept's genesis: "Early in my career, I realized the only way I would ever prove myself was to create my own role in my own script. But I had so many ideas in my head, I couldn't focus on any one. To cheer myself up, I took the last of my entertainment money and went to see the Ali-Wepner fight on closed circuit TV. [Chuck] Wepner, a battle bruising club fighter who had never made the big time, was having his show. It wasn't at all regarded as a serious battle. But as the fight progressed, this miracle unfolded. He hung in there. People went absolutely crazy. Wepner went 15 rounds and established himself as one of the few ever to go the distance with the great Ali. We had witnessed an incredible triumph of the human spirit and we loved it. That night, Rocky Balboa was born."

The original Rocky *captured an unprecedented realism in the ring, helped in no small way by the introduction of the Steadicam.*

Making the Movie

In many ways, the constraints imposed on *Rocky* by its low budget turned out to be blessings in disguise. The filmmakers were forced into finding creative solutions to problems that would otherwise have been solved by money. The result was a very original movie. Chartoff notes, "*Rocky* was great fun to shoot. In part, because we had to shoot it for a million dollars, it ended up having the qualities it did. I think if we had too much money, it may not have been the same film. We never would have hired Bill Conti at that point if someone had given us five million to make the picture; we'd have gone with some standard composer who played it safe rather than played it this way. We didn't even have an art director until two weeks before the end of the picture, and he got an Academy Award nomination. The union forced us to have one. Rather than saying production was hard, in retrospect, I would say it was an opportunity." Director John G. Avildsen adds that the low budget presented a number of challenges. For instance, the ice skating scene between Rocky and Adrian was supposed to have dozens of extras, which the production couldn't afford. One brainstorm later, the decision was made to get Rocky and Adrian alone on the ice. "We had a number of instances where we didn't have the money and we had to come up with other schemes, and it always made it better. Instead of despairing, you say, 'How do we turn this to our advantage?'"

John Avildsen. Director of Rocky *and* Rocky V.

The Cast

Chosen to play Rocky's trainer, Mickey, was veteran actor Burgess Meredith. Says Avildsen, "He read a scene and I said, 'Do it your own way.' They did and when Rocky is walking away dejected, and Burgess yells, 'Hey, did you ever think about retiring?' Stallone doesn't know what to say to him, so he says, 'No,' and Burgess says, 'Well, start thinking about it.' That's how he got the job." The role of Rocky's best friend, Paulie, went to Burt Young. Smiles Chartoff, "Irwin and I had worked with him on *The Gambler* and we knew he was perfect." Carl Weathers was picked for the role of heavyweight champ Apollo Creed. "He hadn't done much acting," Avildesen admits, "but he had a great spirit and a lot of arrogance. He didn't know Sylvester had written it, he thought he was an actor on the film and started complaining about him. He didn't think Sylvester was very good and was very brash, which Sylvester loved." And, finally, Talia Shire was cast in the pivotal role of Rocky's love interest (and Paulie's sister), Adrian. The producers were having difficulty in casting the role, until Shire turned up for audition. Enthuses Chartoff, "The moment we saw her—at least as far as I was concerned—there was no question that Talia was absolutely the right person."

This poster features a scene from a climactic moment of the film that was ultimately cut.

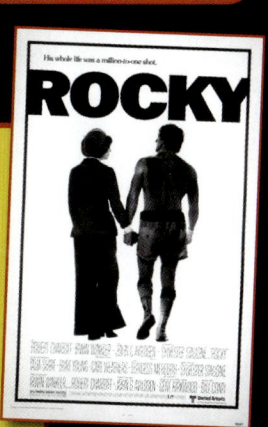

Acclaim

Rocky won Oscars for Directing (Avildsen), Editing (Richard Halsey and Scott Conrad), and Best Picture in 1976. Says Chartoff, "We thought *Network* was going to sweep, which made the win sweeter." Avildsen adds, "Rocky was the perfect fairy tale, and for us, too. The Academy Awards was a shock; a most amazing surprise." Sylvester Stallone sums up exactly what it was that made *Rocky* such a huge hit: "The film really has an impact in the sense that Rocky goes into the fight knowing he's going to lose, which is the most extraordinary act of heroism. It's all about idealism and I wasn't as aware of it at the time as I am now. That is what has endured. It's not that Rocky is the most finely-crafted film of all time or the finest performance ever. It just somehow touched a nerve that every one of us somehow can relate to."

Rocky *wins Best Picture, and producers Robert Chartoff and Irwin Winkler bring Sylvester Stallone to the stage.*

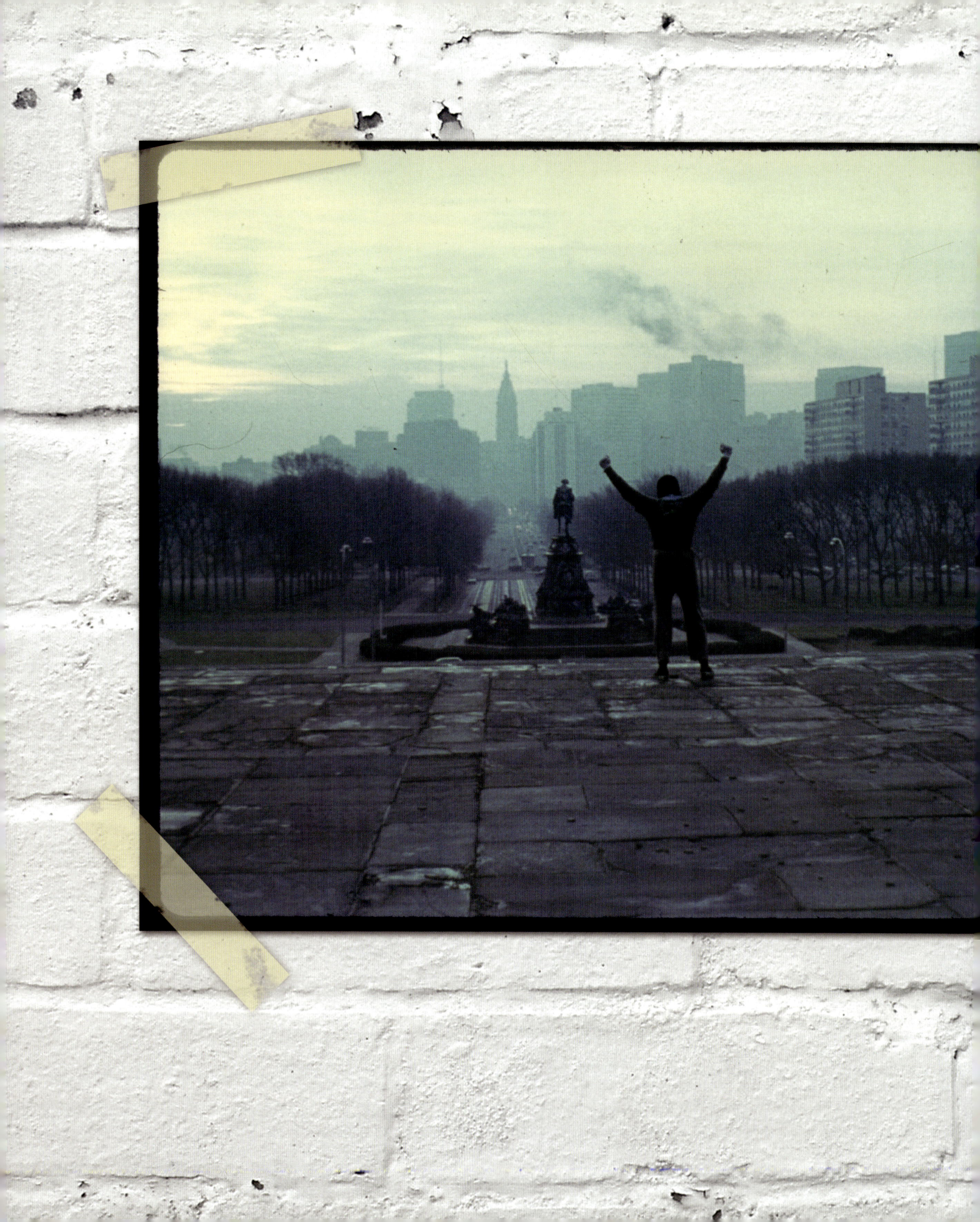

ROCKY

IN 1976, AMERICA NEEDED someone to believe in; a hero who could help them put the pain of the Vietnam War and the betrayal of the Watergate scandal behind them. With the country celebrating its Bicentennial, the time was right for a resurgence of national pride. But the American people desperately needed an icon that could restore their faith in the human spirit, and that is precisely what they got with Sylvester Stallone's portrayal of boxer Rocky Balboa. *Rocky* not only scored a heavyweight hit in that year's Academy Award winner for Best Picture, but, more importantly, the Italian Stallion captured the hearts and imaginations of not just Americans, but people all over the world. Audiences were suddenly jarred into recognizing the importance of not letting life crush you down, of believing in yourself even when the world seems to have given up on you. Of proving your own self-worth. Above all, of going the distance.

The Italian Stallion

> "YOU WEREN'T BORN WITH MUCH OF A BRAIN, SO YOU BETTER LEARN TO USE YOUR BODY."
> ROCKY'S FATHER

ROBERT "ROCKY" BALBOA—the self-proclaimed "Italian Stallion"—had concluded that the chances of making his mark on the world as a boxer were a million to one. Other men might have been crushed under the weight of those odds, yet for Rocky that one-in-a-million shot was enough to keep him going through the toughest of times. Born in 1946 and raised on the mean streets of Philadelphia, Rocky had taken his father's words of advice to heart, and at the age of 16 he thought he had found his purpose in life when he discovered a talent for boxing. Taking his boxing name from personal hero and former champ Rocky Marciano, he began pursuing his newly discovered dream. But the going was far from easy, and the big-hearted tough guy found it impossible to get anyone to take him seriously. More importantly, as the years went by it became painfully obvious that local amateur bouts simply didn't offer enough cash for him to survive. Rocky had no choice but to turn to a less desirable source of income—working for loan shark Tony Gazzo.

Underground Contender

By November of 1975, Rocky's biggest claim to fame was as a frequent winner in sleazy, borderline underground boxing matches with no-name opponents like Spider-Rico. Rocky tried to put his heart into every one of these bouts, but found it frustrating as he instinctively knew that he was better than this; that he could offer the world—and himself—more if he could just get a shot at something greater. His fear was that at the age of 29 his pugilistic clock was ticking and that the opportunity would never come.

ROCKY THE ENFORCER

Rocky's boxing prowess impressed Tony Gazzo, who felt that the fighter would be an effective debt collector. Needing the cash, Rocky accepted the job, though it was a difficult role to play given his innate sense of right and wrong. As it turned out, Rocky's sheer physical presence was intimidating enough to ensure that most people paid what they owed. Rocky refused to break the thumbs of those who couldn't pay up, as ordered by Gazzo, instead he left them with the parting words "You should have planned ahead." They rarely missed a payment again.

Final Fight
Rocky's November 1975 bout with Spider-Rico was to be his last amateur fight. In it, Rocky barely managed a victory, and then only after a head-butt from his opponent sent him into a rage. At this low point, there was no way Rocky could have imagined that the opportunity of a lifetime was just around the corner.

Poor Reward
People often asked Rocky what payback he received for "getting his head busted open" in the ring by the likes of Spider-Rico. He had the answer the night of his victory: $65. From this meager amount he had to pay $15 for his locker, $5 for his shower and towel, and seven percent sales tax. That left him taking home just $40.55.

Paulie

"I'M HAVIN' A BAD DAY." Paulie
"YOU'RE ALWAYS HAVING A BAD DAY." Rocky

Paulie Pennino refused to accept the general consensus that he was a loser. True, he was kind of crude and unpolished. He didn't have the best job in the world either, and he didn't make a lot of money. But people needed him. Could a loser look after his painfully shy sister, Adrian, the way he did? Could a loser be best friends with soon-to-be somebody Rocky Balboa? Maybe they did need him, but what Paulie couldn't admit to himself was that maybe he needed them more. Years earlier Paulie and Rocky had been drawn together by the outside world's views of them as misfits, and bonded over their conviction that they could be so much more—if only they were given the chance. The coming years would be filled with amazing highs and unbelievable lows, but through it all the duo would somehow remain the best of friends.

PAULIE'S WORLD

Employed at the Shamrock Meat Packers, Paulie was always looking for a way out. And though his friendship with Rocky was genuine—no question about that—a part of him also felt that somehow, someway, Rocky could be his ticket to a better life. When Rocky began working for loan shark Tony Gazzo, Paulie begged him to put a good word to Gazzo, feeling that he too would make a great collector. And when Apollo Creed's people came calling, Paulie tried to get involved, at first wanting to help Rocky train, then wanting to handle his P.R. He ultimately settled on making an arrangement in which Rocky's robe would bear the Shamrock logo. As Rocky revealed to Mickey, "Paulie gets three grand, I get the robe." Mickey's reply: "Shrewd."

Highs and Lows
On the surface, the crude, boorish Paulie and the inarticulate but earnest Rocky seemed to have little in common. At this stage of their lives, Paulie and Rocky had no idea of the incredible changes that were in store for both of them over the course of the next decade.

Paulie's reaction to most situations was to get angry: "I'd like to kill the friggin' moron who broke the mirror."

Paulie was indirectly responsible for one of Rocky's early training methods: punching frozen racks of beef.

"You wanna hit me?" Paulie asks. "Come on! I'll break both your arms so they don't work for ya!"

JEALOUS GUY

One drawback of Rocky's mounting success, and something that would become more of a problem as the years went on, was Paulie's jealousy of Rocky. In the beginning everything was fine, the two friends looked out for each other as they struggled to make their mark in life. Paulie felt that the playing field between them was level. But as time passed and Rocky's status in life changed, Paulie grew fearful that his friend would somehow leave him behind. It was only when he listened to Rocky's advice to believe in himself and not depend on others that Paulie eventually changed his attitude.

SOUL MATES

True love had eluded Rocky for most of his life. While his looks had made him popular with women, no genuine relationships had developed, and he had begun to think that he would have to rely on boxing to give him the fulfillment that he craved in life. But all that changed the day he met his best friend Paulie's sister, Adrian, at the local pet store where she worked. Suffering from acute shyness, plainly dressed, and adorned in horn-rimmed glasses, Adrian could hardly be called every man's dream woman. But as far as Rocky was concerned, he had found his soul mate. He just had to convince Adrian of that.

Adrian

"SHE'S GOT GAPS, I GOT GAPS. TOGETHER WE FILL GAPS." Rocky

ADRIAN HAD COME TO ACCEPT the likelihood she would be alone for the rest of her life. But maybe it was a self-fulfilling prophecy. By not believing any man would be interested in her, she did everything she could—lack of make-up, hair styling, or decent clothing—to ensure that no man was. So when Rocky began to pay her attention, Adrian couldn't understand it. What did this ruggedly handsome (if a little dangerous-looking) guy see in her? Nevertheless, she had to admit to herself that the attraction was mutual, though she was too insecure to respond to him. In fact, if not pushed into it by Paulie, she never would have gone out with Rocky on that Thanksgiving night in 1975 and they certainly wouldn't have ended up being the only people on the ice at the skating rink. It was there that Adrian discovered the depths of Rocky's vulnerability and for the first time had the courage to admit her own. Soon both of them realized that somehow each made up for what the other lacked. On a personal level, Rocky made Adrian understand that he didn't regard her shyness as a disease. How a guy who lived his life punching other men into oblivion could be so sensitive was a conundrum she never quite got her brain around.

FIRST KISS

Adrian was reluctant to go back to Rocky's apartment following their first date, but his respectful demeanor convinced her that everything was going to be okay. She felt she could trust him, despite his reputation as a fighter and enforcer for Tony Gazzo. When she gave in to her attraction for him and they embraced for the first time, their desire for each other ignited almost instantly. "I wanna kiss you," said Rocky. "You don't have to kiss me back if you don't wanna." But she did, and it was the start of a passionate relationship that lasted for the rest of her life.

New Relationship

Rocky and Adrian's relationship blossomed very quickly—probably faster than either one of them could have anticipated. Amazing really, considering that their relationship began with Rocky's visits to the pet store where he would offer up one lame joke after another, inevitably bringing a slight smile to Adrian's lips. Despite initial opposition from Paulie, Adrian soon moved in to Rocky's apartment.

Rocky bought his goldfish and turtles from Adrian.

As a special surprise, Adrian bought the dog Butkus from the pet shop for Rocky.

Apollo Creed

"APOLLO CREED MEETS THE ITALIAN STALLION. NOW THAT SOUNDS LIKE A DAMN MONSTER MOVIE." APOLLO CREED

BY THE TIME that Rocky Balboa entered his life, Apollo Creed had already defended his World Heavyweight title forty six times and had, whether he wanted to admit it or not, become complacent. When his original opponent, Mac Lee Green, dropped out of their Bicentennial fight due to an injured left hand, the only thing that concerned Creed was the embarrassment canceling the bout would cause him. With no other ranked fighters ready to take him on, Creed, a born showman, hit on a novel idea—he would fight a local underdog instead. The ideal underdog turned out to be a certain Rocky Balboa. Apollo knew that America had been discovered by an Italian, and chose Balboa purely because his nickname—the Italian Stallion—seemed so appropriate on "the country's biggest birthday." Creed dismissed warnings from his advisors about fighting a southpaw like Rocky. Other fighters might find left-handers threw their timing out, but Apollo Creed didn't worry about that. All he concerned himself with was the public-relations opportunities such an entertaining match-up would provide.

EARLY DAYS

At the beginning of his career, Apollo was never complacent. Although he appeared to take things lightly and made a real show of any bout he was involved with, Apollo trained as hard as he possibly could. He saw each opponent for what they were: a threat to his title and his place in history. For many years Apollo had what he would later describe as the "eye of the tiger"—once he was inside the ropes his frivolity would disappear and be replaced by the ferocious, business-like attitude of a world-class fighter.

LORD OF THE RING

Getting into the ring with an unknown fighter like Rocky Balboa was never supposed to be anything more than an exhibition match, a publicity stunt. But eventually the bout would make Apollo realize just how important it was for him to be in the ring, and how integral to his life the chanting of the crowd and the thrill of the fight were. The idea of retirement was unimaginable to him and it was something that he tried to avoid thinking about. Later in life he would come to realize that boxers are like warriors, and without a war to fight then a warrior might as well be dead.

Apollo's Plan

When Mac Lee Green dropped out of the World Heavyweight title contest, the Creed camp failed to find any other opponents available to fight at short notice. Apollo refused to accept that five weeks wasn't enough time for a rival boxer to get into shape. "They're making excuses," he exclaimed, "so they don't have to be the chump to get whipped in front of the whole civilized world!" He then hit on the idea of opening up the competition to a local fighter.

After coming up with his idea, Apollo searched the boxing registry to find a likely candidate.

Rocky's nickname, the Italian Stallion, appealed to Apollo. "I'll drop him in three," he promised.

Apollo's handlers grew concerned watching footage of Rocky punching away at a slab of beef.

Apollo was told that his idea was very American. "No," he countered. "It's very smart."

Rising to the Challenge

"APOLLO LIKES YOU. HE WANTS TO FIGHT YOU." George Jergens

WHEN ROCKY HEARD promoter George Jergens had been asking about him, he thought he knew why. Word was going around that Jergens was looking for sparring partners for Apollo Creed, and Rocky assumed that was where the promoter's interest lay. Walking into Jergen's office, he launched into his well-rehearsed speech accepting the expected offer. It was then that Jergens dropped his bombshell: what he was actually offering Rocky was a chance to fight Apollo Creed for the World Heavyweight Championship. A stunned Rocky responded with the first word that came to mind: "No." As he saw it, Apollo was way out of his league. But Jergens was nothing if not a persuasive man. Appealing to the fighter's sense of pride, he explained that the champ wanted to to prove that America was truly a land of opportunity by giving an unknown a shot at the title, and had personally chosen Rocky to be that unknown. "It's the chance of a lifetime. You can't pass it by," Jergens urged. And Rocky realized that he was right.

PRESS CONFERENCE

At the pre-fight press conference with Apollo Creed, Rocky revealed that he had "invented" the name Italian Stallion some eight years earlier. Creed, true to his usual form, aimed a series of jibes at the challenger. "Rocky, ain't you Italian?" he asked. When Balboa nodded, Apollo quipped, "That means if he can't fight... I bet he can cook." The comment drew a roar of laughter from the gathered reporters. Watching a TV newscast of the conference later in his living room with Paulie, Rocky shrugged off all the cheap shots, claiming that they didn't bother him. But later, when he was alone with Adrian, he admitted that some of the jibes had hit home.

Rocky's Doubts

Unable to sleep, Rocky went over to the Philadelphia Spectrum, the venue for his fight with Creed. There he stared at the posters, one of Apollo and one of himself. A year earlier he had been taking on opponents like Spider-Rico with little hope of achieving anything better. Yet here he was, on the threshhold of what should have been a dream come true, and he was terrified. He was not scared of losing to Creed—that seemed an inevitability—but of simply not measuring up to being the man he had always felt that he was.

Rocky was surprised to find Jergens was at the venue as well. "The poster is wrong," Rocky told him, "I'm wearing white pants with a red stripe." The image showed the opposite—red pants with a white stripe.

It really doesn't matter, does it?" Jergens tried reassuring him. "I'm sure you're going to give us a great show." Details meant nothing to Jergens; the entertainment value of the "show" was his sole concern.

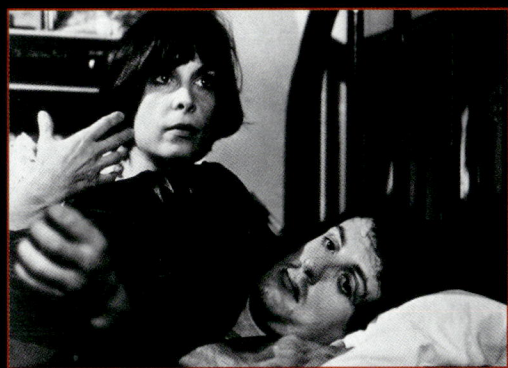

Back home, Rocky gently awakened Adrian to express his ultimate hope: "If that bell rings and I'm still standing, I'm gonna know for the first time in my life that I weren't just another bum from the neighborhood."

ROCKY'S MENTOR

There hadn't been much of a father figure in Rocky's life, his own having taken off years earlier. The closest he came to one was in his relationship with seventy six-year-old local gym owner Mickey Goldmill. Ironic, considering the acrimony between the two men in the first six years they had known each other. It took Rocky a long time to realize that what he had at first interpreted as complete disrespect was actually Mick's disgust with Rocky for wasting his life away fighting "bums" and working for Tony Gazzo.

Mickey and the Gym

"YOU CAN'T BUY WHAT I'M GONNA GIVE YOU." Mickey

MICKEY WASN'T THE ONLY character from Rocky's past to show up at his apartment following the announcement of his fight with Creed. In recent days all sorts of "old friends" had attempted to re-enter his life. But with Mickey, things were different. Only a short time before, he had kicked Rocky out of his locker at the boxing gym to make room for an up-and-coming fighter named Dipper, essentially condemning Rocky to what he called "Skid Row." Yet here he was, asking Rocky to let him be his manager. The nerve of the man was something else. Rocky was disgusted at Mickey's change of attitude toward him now there was a sniff of glory, besides, he had already decided to go it alone and manage himself. But the old timer launched into his sales pitch regardless, offering Rocky the benefits of a lifetime's boxing experience. "I got all this knowledge—I got it up here now and I want to give it to you," he insisted. Mickey pleaded his case with increasing desperation until Rocky's pent-up resentment finally exploded in a torrent of abuse. It wasn't until Mickey had left the apartment that—his anger spent—the fighter began to have second thoughts.

A NEW BEGINNING

Rocky's decision to follow his gut instincts and let Mickey manage him ended up, strangely enough, having a positive effect on both of their lives. For Rocky, it was an opportunity to reach his potential in a way he never had before. And for Mickey, it provided a focus in life, allowing him to show his love for the sport that had meant so much to him, as well as to taste a bit of glory. Mickey believed that when people lose the things they care about one by one, they ultimately lose their reason to live. In training an unknown boxer like Rocky to be a contender for the World Heavyweight title, he found a reason not just to live, but to put a lifetime of boxing experience to the best possible use.

Mickey's Request

It took every bit of restraint Rocky could muster not to physically toss Mickey out of his apartment when he showed up requesting to be his manager. This guy had treated him like garbage, yet he was here asking Rocky for something. Rocky's resentment at years of bad treatment exploded into a full-blown tirade, "I needed your help about ten years ago, right? You never helped me none. You didn't care. I asked, but you never heard nothin'."

To prove he was the real deal, Mickey showed Rocky a photo of himself in his boxing prime.

"At least you had a prime, Mick," Rocky screamed. "I ain't had no prime. I ain't had nothin'!"

Mickey left the apartment a broken man, with Rocky's booming rant echoing in his ears.

Moments later, Rocky caught up with Mickey. The fighter had decided to give him a chance.

The Training

"YOU'RE GONNA EAT LIGHTNING AND YOU'RE GONNA CRAP THUNDER!" MICKEY

Throughout his amateur career—if "career" was the right word for it—Rocky's idea of preparing for a fight was to kick off the day before dawn with a cup of raw eggs, follow that up with a few sets of sit-ups and push-ups, and from there set off on a jog through the neighborhood. His end goal was inevitably the top of the steps leading to the Philadelphia Art Museum, although he seldom made it all the way up and the few times he did his ribs were racked with terrible pain. It never occurred to Rocky to vary this routine and he had every intention of sticking to it in the run-up to his exhibition match with Heavyweight Champion Apollo Creed. In the end, Mickey became the light that illuminated Rocky's darkness, showing the would-be World Heavyweight Championship contender just how much there was to learn and exactly what he would have to do to prepare for his match with Creed. Mickey's training program was to regularly stretch Rocky to the limits of his endurance, but the results would be worth all the pain. When Mickey was through with him, Rocky would be tough enough to "spit nails."

PUNCHING POWER

Rocky's punching power showed itself in spectacular style on a visit to Paulie at his place of employment, the Shamrock Meat Plant. After suffering a series of off-color comments from Paulie about his relationship with Adrian, Rocky let loose his anger on a full rack of frozen ribs. Jab after jab he reduced the meat to a pulp, the sound of snapping, frozen bones clearly audible. Stunned, Paulie tried to dissipate the tension with a joke: "You do that to Apollo Creed and they'll put us in jail for murder." Rocky would continue this method of practice until Paulie, courting publicity, brought a TV crew down to the meat plant to interview the fighter.

A NEW APPROACH

Under Mickey's instruction, Rocky began training in an all-new way. Mickey recognized that Rocky needed balance and had a string tied to both of the fighter's ankles, with about two feet of slack between them. "Marciano had the same problem," Mickey pointed out, "and this string cured it. The idea is that if you can move and you can hit without breaking the string, you got balance. You become a very dangerous person."

No Pain, No Gain

Rocky had never before felt pain like the pain he experienced under Mickey's tutelage. But he also recognized that with the passing of each day, he was getting stronger and more prepared to get into the boxing ring with Apollo Creed.

A cup of raw eggs was Rocky's idea of a healthy nutrition shake.

Local people got accustomed to seeing Rocky on his daily runs, and started cheering him on.

To build up Rocky's strength and balance, Mickey got him on a program of grueling one-armed push-ups.

Rocky victorious—the boxer finally makes it to the top of the steps!

The Fight

"HE DOESN'T KNOW IT'S A SHOW! HE THINKS IT'S A DAMN FIGHT! FINISH THIS BUM AND LET'S GO HOME." Duke (Apollo's Trainer)

IN THE SPIRIT of America's Bicentennial celebrations, Apollo came into the ring at the Philadelphia Spectrum wearing a pair of red, white, and blue trunks. He wasn't expecting much from this match—a bit of sweat maybe, but mostly some first-class entertainment for the millions of fans who were watching ringside, at home, and around the world. As far as Apollo was concerned, this Italian Stallion was a gimmick that would be quickly disposed of for the entertainment of the crowd.

Round 1
At the sound of the bell, Rocky and Apollo moved toward each other and began to fight. Right away, Apollo started dancing around the ring in his trademark style, shooting out jabs which connected with Rocky's face, and made his head snap back in response. It looked as if this was going to be a be a one-sided fight—until Rocky struck back with such force that it sent Apollo sprawling to the canvas. "Creed is down! What a surprise this is!" offered a dumbstruck announcer. Barely avoiding the ten-count, Apollo got to his feet and for the first time began taking Rocky seriously, breaking his nose with a right jab just as the round ended.

Round 2
Despite his broken nose, Rocky found himself in awe of Apollo, noting to Mickey, "The guy is great." At the same time, Apollo's team was digesting the fact that they had seriously underestimated Rocky Balboa. As round two commenced, Apollo came roaring back, hoping to make quick work of the so-called Italian Stallion and prove to everyone that the first round knock-down was just a lucky punch. But Rocky resolutely refused to go down. Instead, he came back with a ferocity that absolutely stunned the champion—trapping him against the ropes and unleashing blow after blow.

Round 3
Apollo pummeled Rocky, feeling for the first time that this unknown southpaw from Philly might have a chance. He was rapidly drawing the conclusion that no matter what he threw out, his opponent would just refuse to fall.

Round 4-12
One round gave way to another as the two fighters continued their battle. Apollo found himself gaining not only a respect but a genuine fear of Rocky Balboa's potential. And it was this fear that fueled his attacks; that fed his need to do away with the underdog who was gaining in favor with the crowd. But Rocky refused to cooperate, taking everything the champ had to offer. Battered and bloodied, Rocky fought back, giving as good as he got.

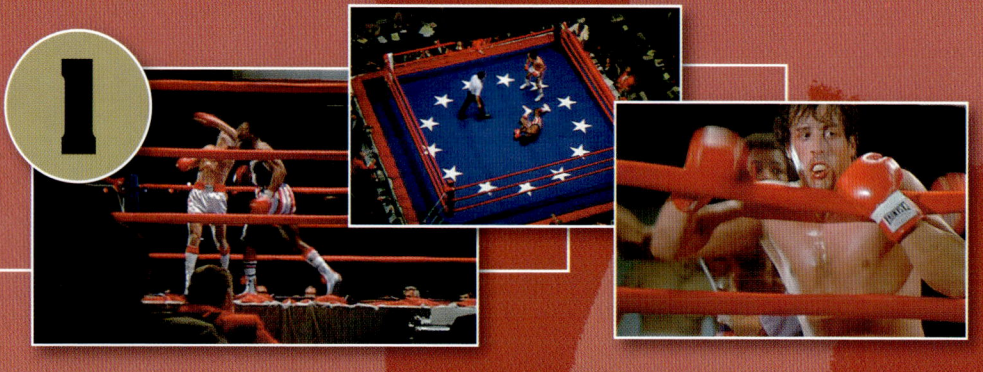

"THIS IS THE FIRST TIME THE CHAMPION'S BEEN KNOCKED DOWN." Announcer

"ROCKY IS LIKE A BULL IN A CHINA CLOSET." Announcer

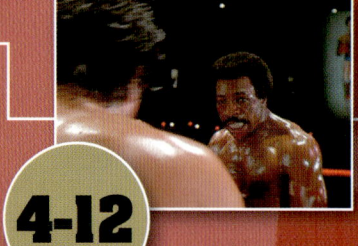

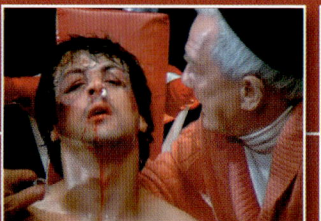

"HE'S TAUNTING ROCKY TO COME ON IN." Announcer

Round 13

Not even the best odds-makers had expected a twist of this nature. No-one imagined that this fight between the World Heavyweight Champion and an unknown boxer would actually go all the way. For this reason, not only was it shocking that there was a 13th round and that both men were still standing, but also that Apollo's face had become as swollen and bloodied as Rocky's. Coming into the fight, Apollo's record stood at forty six undefeated bouts, so no one could have predicted such an outcome when the "monster movie" fight of "Apollo Creed Meets The Italian Stallion" was announced.

Round 14

It was only a matter of time before one of the boxers fell, but which one? The answer came suddenly as Apollo delivered a combination that sent Rocky to the canvas. Dazed and disoriented, Rocky knew he had to get back to his feet, despite Mickey's advice to stay down. Driven by an innate need to prove himself, Balboa managed to stand. He narrowly avoided the ten-count, as Apollo's had in round one. Rocky motioned for Creed to continue. The dumbfounded and exhausted champ obliged, only to receive a series of devastating blows to the ribs.

> "APOLLO'S CLEARLY PROTECTING HIS RIGHT SIDE, HIS RIBS." Announcer

> "LOOK AT THE BLOOD COMING OUT OF HIM! HE'S SPITTING UP BLOOD." Announcer

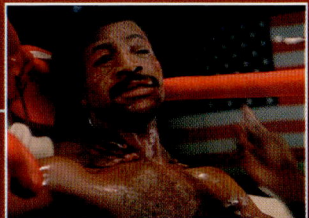

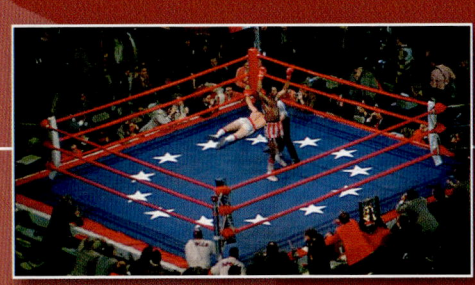

Unbelievably, Apollo has a real fight on his hands.

Apollo unleashes another punishing right hook.

Bloodied and hurting like hell, Rocky goes the distance.

Rocky protects his body with his right hand.

Apollo's Stars and Stripes trunks show his patriotism.

The Final Round

"AIN'T GONNA BE NO REMATCH." Apollo
"DON'T WANT ONE." Rocky

YEARS AFTER ROCKY'S fight with Apollo Creed, Mickey admitted to Balboa that his battle with the champ should have killed him. If Mickey had confessed his concerns when Rocky and his opponent were squaring up for the start of the fifteenth and final round, there's no doubt that the battered and exhausted Rocky would have believed him. Anyone watching the fight would have thought the same. There was simply no way that Rocky should still have been standing. But he was, and he was ready to go all the way. In Rocky's mind quitting was not an option, no matter how tough it got. He had to prove that he could go the distance with Apollo, not for Mickey, not even for Adrian—but for himself.

TRUE CONTENDER

When Apollo faced Rocky at the start of the fifteenth round, he couldn't quite believe what was happening to him. Forcing himself to hide the pain he was feeling from his ribs, which had undoubtedly been broken in their last exchange, he stepped forward ready for one last effort to turn the match in his favor. He was overwhelmed with the feeling that everything he had spent his life working toward, all that he had achieved, was on the verge of slipping between his gloves. And it was all because of a pug from Philly who, in his arrogance, he had believed didn't deserve to be in the same ring as him. Apollo had no choice but to admit now, at least to himself, that Rocky Balboa had proven himself a more than worthy challenger for the title of World Heavyweight Champion.

Apollo knew that this was his last chance to turn the tide. Everything he had fought for hung in the balance.

The champ hit Rocky with everything that he could muster in what would turn out to be a final combination.

But Rocky just kept on coming, driven by an unseen force that seemed almost supernatural in its relentlessness.

Rocky landed punch after punch. All that prevented Apollo from hitting the canvas were the ropes and the final bell.

"THEY LOOK LIKE THEY'VE BEEN IN A WAR, THESE TWO."
— COMMENTATOR

Beyond exhausted, both men proclaimed to the world that they weren't interested in a rematch.

A stunned media demanded interviews, asking Rocky if he thought that he had won the fight.

A moment later, the world had its answer: Apollo was the winner by a split decision. But Rocky couldn't care less.

Adrian slipped into the ring and embraced Rocky. That feeling, at that moment in time, meant more to him than anything.

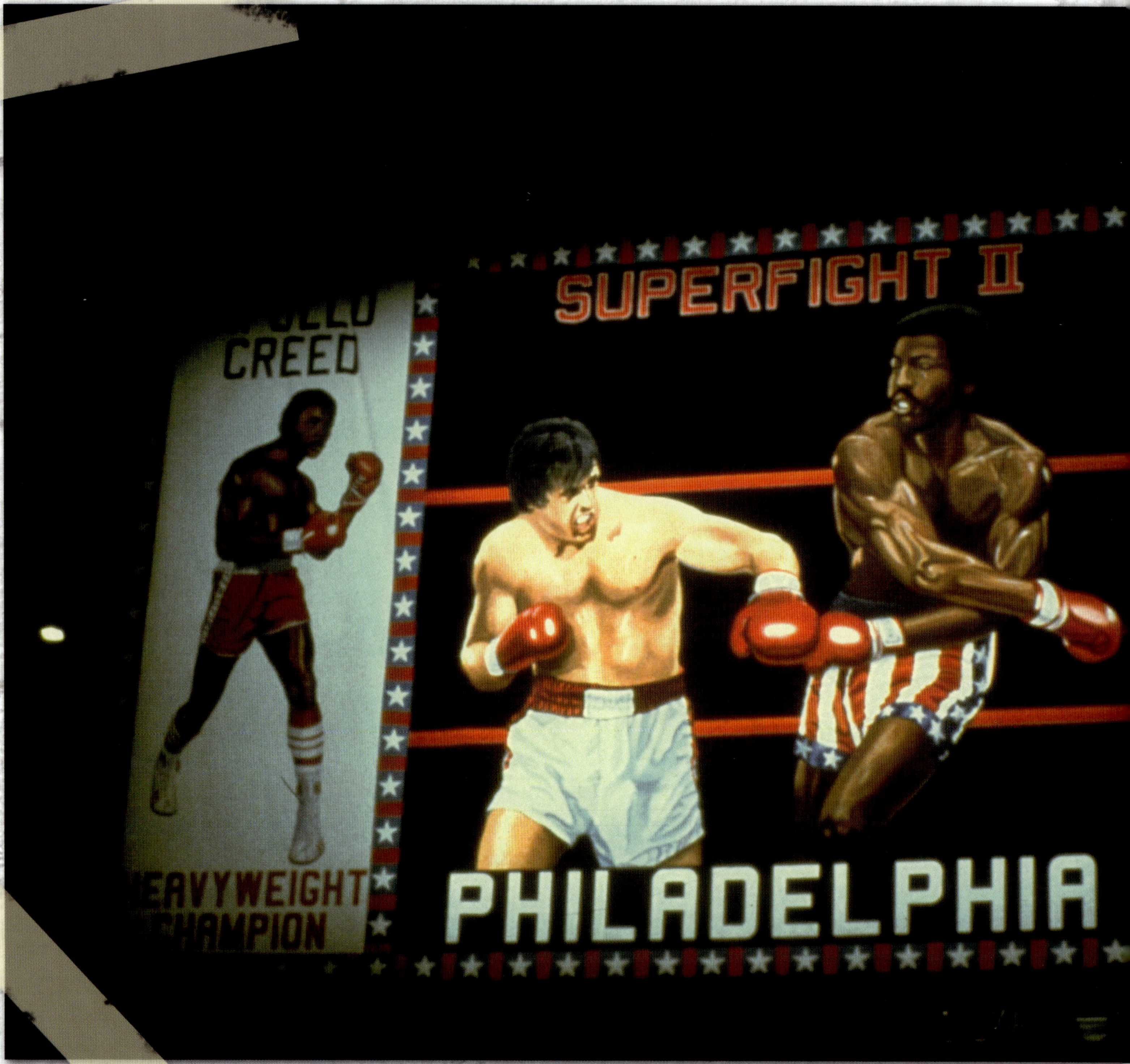
CREED
SUPERFIGHT II
PHILADELPHIA

ROCKY II

BY 1979, THE ITALIAN STALLION was ready for a rematch with Apollo Creed in much the way that his creator, Sylvester Stallone, was ready for another assault on Hollywood. Although the success of the original film had catapulted Stallone to the top of the superstar tree, a lackluster box office performance from the follow-up would be a major threat to his place there. In a sense, both Stallone and Rocky were driven by the desire to prove that they were more than just a one-hit wonder. Thus fired up, the resulting movie was a triumph and stood apart from most sequel fare in an era when follow-ups usually failed to live up to their hype. Outside of *The Godfather Part II*, no sequel was embraced by the public in the way that *Rocky II* was. And for good reason—at its heart, *Rocky II* was a necessary follow-up, exploring the impact events of the first film had on the cast of characters, and allowing them to move on to the next stage of their lives. Stallone was similarly moving on, this time directing the movie as well as writing and starring in it.

Gloves and Marriage

"STALLION, YOU'RE THE LUCKIEST MAN ALIVE." Apollo
"DO I LOOK LUCKY?" Rocky

THERE WAS A MOMENT in his fight with Apollo when Rocky truly thought he was dying. In all his years of fighting, he'd never experienced such pain and exhaustion. Yet at the same time he was driven by a stubborn need to stay on his feet; to see this thing through to the end, knowing that he would never have a chance like this again. The entire experience was beyond anything Rocky could have anticipated, and that dreamlike feeling continued after the fight, as he arrived at the hospital. Ushered via wheelchair into the main lobby, he was amazed to find himself met by a sea of reporters, all clamoring for his attention and demanding answers from this underdog who by rights shouldn't have made it past the first round. They were hailing Rocky as some kind of miracle man. Apollo Creed, witnessing the scenes from his own wheelchair, had to agree with them.

NEW CHALLENGE

Apollo liked to make an entrance, and the injuries inflicted on him by Rocky were not going to stop him now. Having recovered from the bout of humility that marked the end of their fight, he was back to his usual loudmouthed self, practically climbing out of his wheelchair and challenging Rocky to a rematch—"anyplace, anytime"—right in front of everyone. Rocky was stunned, as both men had agreed that there would be no rematch. Things weren't helped when Mickey added another blow to Apollo's bruised ego, claiming that despite the judges decision, Rocky was the true winner of the fight. Reissuing his challenge, Apollo was effectively silenced when Rocky announced that there would be no rematch. He was retiring.

"APOLLO, DID YOU GIVE ME YOUR BEST?" Rocky
"YEAH." Apollo
"THANK YOU." Rocky

When Rocky proposed to Adrian at the zoo, she didn't need time to consider. Her answer was an unhesitating "Yes."

Going Home

His injuries healed, Rocky got on with the business of settling down to married life with Adrian. Not used to life working out for him, he didn't really know how to handle it now that things seemed to be going so well. He had gotten into the ring with the heavyweight champ and, against all odds, had proven himself by going the distance. Then he had asked the love of his life for her hand in marriage, and she had agreed. Now, with the couple ready to embark on their new lives together, things seemed almost too good to be true. Adrian felt exactly the same way; just a year earlier she was convinced she would be alone for the rest of her life, and yet here she was, starting the next chapter as Mrs. Rocky Balboa.

"IF I'D KNOWN YOU WERE SO LIGHT, I WOULD'VE CARRIED YOU EVERYWHERE." Rocky

The Wedding

The wedding may have been neither big nor glamorous, but it was perfect by Rocky and Adrian's standards. With Father Carmine officiating over the small, intimate ceremony, witnesses to their union included Mickey (who was quick to hurry back to the gym to check out some contenders), Paulie, and Rocky's former employer, loan shark Tony Gazzo. Chatting to Rocky after the wedding, Gazzo advised the fighter to put his money into condominiums because they were "safe." "Condominiums?" replied Rocky, "I never use 'em."

As things turned out, the marriage of Rocky and Adrian would indeed last until death parted them.

Rocky reassured Adrian when she confided her fear that he would one day get tired of her.

Money and Losing It

"YO, ADRIAN, DO YOU LIKE TO HAVE A GOOD TIME? THEN YOU NEED A GOOD WATCH." Rocky

ROCKY AND ADRIAN believed that their love would carry them through life: never having had any money, they didn't attach much significance to it. Then, with Rocky's fight with Apollo Creed netting him over $37,000, they suddenly found themselves rich and Rocky seemed to become fiscally unhinged, launching on an incredible spending spree. Adrian attempted to slow him down, but instead found herself pulled along in the Italian Stallion's wake. Among their quickly acquired possessions: a new car, expensive jewelry (including some for Butkus the dog), a fur coat, and a new house. Inevitably, it wasn't long before the money began to run out, and with Adrian now pregnant, Rocky realized he needed to find a new source of income, fast. A serious eye injury—and his promise to Adrian—meant a return to the ring was out of the question. It seemed the only opportunity on the horizon was the commercials an agent had approached him about while he was in the hospital.

COMMERCIAL FAILURE

It soon became obvious that Rocky's days as a commercial pitch person were limited due to his inability to either read the dummy cards or act. Set to sell aftershave—first in the role of a cave man surrounded by beautiful women and then as a bruised boxer—he ruined take after take by stumbling over his words. Eventually, after hours of humiliation, Rocky found himself fired. Angry at seeing her husband made a fool of, Adrian felt more relief than disappointment.

JOBLESS IN PHILLY

Hoping to better himself, Rocky approached employment offices all around Philadelphia looking for a desk job—something where he could use his brains rather than his muscles. But with his lack of a good education and qualifications, he had nothing to offer a potential employer. A search for something in physical labor proved equally fruitless, so despite her pregnancy Adrian went back to her job in the pet store to make ends meet. Then in an ironic twist of fate, Paulie, who was now working Rocky's job as an enforcer for Gazzo on the docks, got him a job at the meat plant. For a while the job was a lifeline, but before long he was laid off due to cutbacks. It was a desperate situation. Every day the walls were closing in on Rocky a little more.

Back to the Gym

The ticket out of this mess would have been boxing, but Adrian was adamant that that wasn't an option. Nevertheless, Rocky had to admit to himself that he was missing the world of boxing more than he had expected. That, and the fact that he hadn't managed to find anything else, eventually drew him back to Mickey's gym. He had a proposition to make.

Employment agencies advised Rocky to try his hand at fighting again, but he refused to go back on his promise.

Rocky admitted to Mickey that he needed to be around boxing, even if it meant taking a cleaning job in the gym.

The descent from boxing hero to menial worker opened Rocky up to ridicule from other boxers.

Creed vs. the Stallion Chicken

"YOU'RE A DISGRACE TO YOUR PEOPLE!"
APOLLO'S HATE MAIL

WHEN APOLLO CREED held his hand up in victory at the conclusion of his first fight with Rocky, he had no idea that months later he would still be justifying the judges' decision to the world. Hate mail continued to arrive on a daily basis, and the respect he had earned over the years seemed to have vanished overnight. Creed brooded on all this, to the point of neglecting his wife and family. There seemed to be only one way of laying this ghost, and that was by getting back into the ring with Rocky. However, not everyone thought this was a good idea, including Creed's own team, and he began to feel that even his own people doubted him. When asked if he won the fight, Apollo's manager/trainer, Tony, had replied, "You got the decision," which caused Apollo to fairly explode, "Man, I beat him, but I didn't win!"

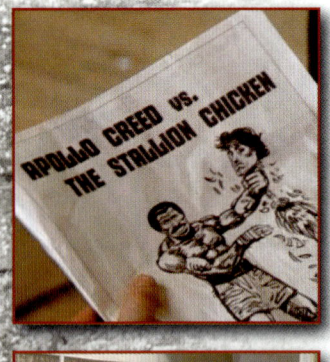

HUMILIATION TACTICS

The biggest roadblock for Apollo was the fact that Rocky had retired, so he launched a public campaign. What the champ didn't know was that Rocky himself was desperate to get back into the ring, and only resisted doing so for Adrian's sake. In truth, he was finding it more and more difficult to ignore Apollo's constant goading in print and on television. Eventually, when Mickey showed up at the Balboa home after a televised assault, proclaiming that they ought to "knock his block off," Rocky, under Adrian's disapproving gaze, responded, "Absolutely."

"YOU GOTTA GET SPEED. DEMON SPEED. SPEED IS WHAT WE NEED. WE NEED GREASY FAST SPEED" Mickey

THE NEED FOR SPEED

Mickey had already decided that Rocky should learn to fight right-handed in order to protect his damaged eye and throw Creed off balance. When he watched film of the first fight with Apollo, he thought that he had pinpointed the other thing that Rocky most needed to survive—speed. From that moment on, everything that they did would be designed to ensure that he could move around the ring and prevent Creed from taking command of it. Among Mickey's old-school methods was the idea of Rocky attempting to catch a chicken in a confined area. Rocky, already in a bad place due to the fact that he and Adrian had barely spoken since his decision to fight Apollo, was dismissive of the whole idea. "I feel like a Kentucky Fried Idiot," he said.

Loss of Faith

Adrian had no idea that her refusal to support Rocky was destroying his faith in himself. His training was completely off and he found himself easily distracted. Noticing this, Mickey tried everything he could to motivate Rocky into getting more serious.

Gym time got harder and harder, reaching a point where even sparring partners were scoring on Rocky.

Frustrated, Rocky told Mick he wanted to go back to hitting the bag left-handed. "If you do," snarled Mickey, "I'll chop it off!"

Thinking he was helping, Paulie went to the pet store to confront Adrian, but the stress sent her into premature labor.

The Vigil

"IF YOU WANNA BLOW THIS THING, THEN WE'LL BLOW IT TOGETHER." Mickey

LIFE CHANGED in an instant. The fight with Apollo meant nothing. Money meant nothing. All that mattered to Rocky was Adrian and their newborn son. Devastated when he learned that the premature labor had plunged Adrian into a coma, Rocky refused to see the baby until he and Adrian could do so together. He had, at least, the comfort of knowing that the child had been born healthy, but the doctors' prognosis for Adrian wasn't as optimistic. As the days passed and Adrian showed no sign of waking, people's concerns began to shift from her to Rocky. Paulie, especially, seemed to be losing hope that his sister would awaken, and feared that if he lost Adrian, he would lose Rocky, too. Perhaps surprizingly, it was Mickey who turned out to be Rocky's greatest source of strength during this agonizing time. Promising to back the fighter up whatever he decided to do—even if that meant pulling out of the fight—he rarely left Rocky's side as he sat by Adrian's bed or prayed in the hospital chapel. His loyalty was something Rocky would not forget.

THE READER

As Adrian lay in a coma, Rocky didn't know where to turn. In the end he did what felt natural: he stayed by his wife's side, hour-after-hour, day-after-day. He prayed at her bedside, he read aloud to her, or he simply sat with her, silently holding her hand. The only time he left Adrian's side was to go to the hospital chapel and pray to God for help. Through his grief, Rocky couldn't help noticing the looks he had started getting from people; looks of sorrow and pity. But he didn't want their sympathy—he knew Adrian would come out of the darkness and they would be together again.

Awakening

Rocky was never sure what finally brought his wife out of her coma. Maybe, during all those hours of reading by her bedside, his familiar voice had kept some vital spark of consciousness alive in her. Or maybe it was his unyielding faith. All he knew was that he had been fitfully sleeping beside Adrian, his head resting on her mattress and his hand clasped around her unmoving one, when he was suddenly alert at the miraculous feeling of her fingers intertwining with his. Raising his head, he watched in wonder as she opened her eyes. "I knew you'd come back," he murmured.

After seeing Rocky Jr. with Adrian for the first time, Rocky told his wife that he would give up his fight with Apollo.

Instead of agreeing, Adrian told him there was only one thing that she wanted him to do for her: "Win!"

Right Hand Man

At first, Rocky thought Mickey's notion of his switching from a Southpaw to a right-handed fighter was ridiculous, but Mickey was convinced that it would be a great way of catching the champ completely off guard.

Mickey's unrelenting training methods required Rocky to lift weights that would have crushed most men.

The need for speed was constantly driven into Rocky's head by Mick. Speed and endurance were everything.

Prior to Adrian's support for the Apollo rematch, Rocky hadn't been able to maintain any sort of rhythm with the punching bag. Now, he seemed unstoppable.

Rocky's Back

"TO PULL THIS MIRACLE OFF, YOU'VE GOT TO CHANGE EVERYTHING." MICKEY

ARMED WITH ADRIAN'S BLESSING and with the bond between himself and Mickey strengthened beyond measure, Rocky's attitude to his rematch with Apollo Creed underwent a complete transformation. Gone was the tentative fighter; the distracted Southpaw who was completely unable to focus on the task at hand. In his place stood the Italian Stallion, who was not only willing to throw everything he had into the fight, but was also driven by an inner need to prove to Adrian that her faith in him had not been in vain. The question on everyone's mind, of course, was whether or not Rocky would be able to prevail in the time that was left. The bottom line was that between his half-hearted training and the trauma with Adrian and the baby, a tremendous amount of time had passed and there was some serious concern over whether—Rocky's raw determination notwithstanding—it was simply too late. Backing out was not an option, not that he would have chosen it even if it was. Rocky realized that there was only one way forward: he had to train harder than he ever had before.

People's Hero

Rocky was an unknown the first time he went up against Apollo, but by the time of the rematch he had become something of a hero to the people of Philadelphia. His morning runs were greeted by crowds of supporters, all cheering on this local boy who was going to take on the world.

Smashing metal in a junkyard was as unique as pounding frozen meat.

Another of Rocky's unorthadox means of building strength and endurance.

Rocky was far from alone climbing the steps to the art museum.

THE CREED FACTOR

Rocky was not alone in his steadfast focus on preparing for the fight. Apollo Creed too, filled with a determination to prove to the world that Rocky had merely gotten lucky a year earlier, would let nothing distract him from his objective. Unlike before their original bout, he wasn't concerning himself with publicity stunts of any kind. This was serious. Rocky Balboa, he commanded himself, must fall and fall quickly. For his part, Rocky had his own need to prove something in this fight—that all Apollo's taunts were groundless, and his near-victory in their original match was not a fluke.

The Rematch

"STICK AND MOVE. THIS MAN IS DANGEROUS." Duke (Apollo's trainer)
"THIS MAN IS DANGEROUS? I'M DANGEROUS." Apollo Creed

The mood surrounding the rematch was completely different to the party atmosphere of the first fight. Apollo had abandoned all sense of frivolity. Gone were the costumes, the wisecracks, the playful taunts. He was there with one purpose only—to prove his supremacy in the sport. As for Rocky, he was determined not to let this second chance slip though his grasp, and above all driven by the need to justify Adrian's faith in him and to do what she requested and win.

Round 1
Right away, Apollo began demonstrating how serious he was by unleashing an unrelenting series of punches that barely gave Rocky a chance to breathe. Somehow, Rocky seemed defenseless against this assault. His switch from Southpaw to right-handed fighter shocked the ringsider commentators, but seemed to have no effect at all on Apollo. None of Rocky's blows seemed to do any damage. After verbally goading him, Apollo delivered a series of punches that sent Rocky to the canvas. Although he quickly got back up, he realized that his nose had been broken again.

"YOU'RE A GREASY-FAST ITALIAN TANK. GO THROUGH! RUN OVER HIM!" Mickey

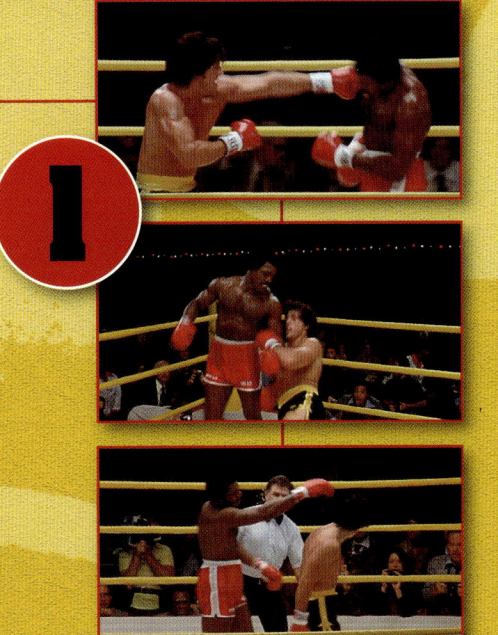

Round 2
Dancing around the ring in classic style, Apollo seemed to be returning to his true nature as a showman. He addressed the ringside photographers, telling them to get their cameras ready, before unleashing more blows—some of them almost theatrically delivered—that sent Rocky to the canvas once again. By the time the count got to "eight," however, Rocky was back on his feet and at last managing to inflict a bit of damage of his own before the bell rang to end the round. Back in his corner, he looked to Mickey and proclaimed, "I ain't going down no more."

Round 3-5
Apollo continued to notch up the points in what was obviously rapidly becoming a one-sided fight. While moving around the ring, Apollo continued to address the crowd, making fun of Rocky and the supposed "skills" at his disposal. Yet despite everything thrown his way, it was undeniable that the Italian Stallion was staying on his feet and seemingly getting stronger.

Round 6-8
While it still seemed to be Apollo's fight, at one point in round six Rocky did manage to get him in the corner to deliver body blows; the change in Apollo's expression betraying the fact that damage was being done. Then, in round eight, Rocky fought back so strongly that for the first time he got the better of Apollo. It was obvious to everyone watching that Creed had lost his first round.

Round 9-10

Rocky, at last, had gotten a foothold in this fight and began a comeback of sorts. While it was clear that Apollo was still in control, the fight had suddenly stopped being so one-sided. Miraculously, Rocky seemed to be gaining strength just as Apollo had begun to slow down. Between rounds Apollo's trainer, Duke, advised him to "Stick and move. This man is breaking you up inside." Yet by the end of the tenth round, Apollo managed to turn things around and Rocky seemed on the verge of collapse, until he was saved by the bell.

Round 11

Rocky spent much of the eleventh through thirteenth rounds in the corner of the ring, being pummeled by Apollo. Using his arms to protect himself as best he could, Rocky was nonetheless subjugated to one brutal body blow after another. Yet still he didn't fall.

Rocky absorbs blow after blow, refusing to fall.

A left hook from Apollo connects with its target.

Round 14

As the bell rang for the penultimate round, both men realized that the only chance for victory—true victory and not just the score of the judges—was for one of them to fall. Completely exhausted, Apollo nonetheless forced himself to keep pushing forward, delivering combinations that still had a powerful effect on his opponent. Rocky, having survived thirteen gruelling rounds, was forced to find deeper and still deeper reserves of strength and determination. Both men were so desperate to triumph over the other that when the final bell rang, they were still exchanging blows.

Everything came down to this moment as Apollo and Rocky stepped forward to engage in their final round.

Rocky resurged with one body blow after another, the force of his punches actually lifting Apollo right off the canvas.

After a final exchange of violent blows, Apollo and Rocky went sprawling simultaneously to the canvas.

With the heavyweight championship title on the line, both men desperately crawled for the ropes.

The Decider

"YOU'RE GOING DOWN!" APOLLO CREED
"UH, UH. NO WAY." ROCKY

AS APOLLO RETURNED to his corner following the conclusion of the 14th round, Duke was practically begging him to stay away from Rocky, to resist the temptation of going for a knockdown. Creed was ahead on points—all he needed to do was keep out of danger and the fight was his. Apollo refused to listen; for him this was about more than a simple points victory. "He's going to fall," he insisted, "It's not going to be like last time." With the ringing of the bell, both men slowly approached the center of the ring, to touch gloves for the last time.

LAST CHANCE

In the opposite corner, Mickey was insisting that Rocky should switch back to Southpaw to keep Apollo off balance, but Rocky was adamant that he would not rely on any sort of trick to win the title. As the bell rang and Apollo came out swinging, there was an instant when he might almost have changed his mind, but a second later something happened—something that felt like history repeating itself. Somehow, in a way that he could never explain, Rocky found a reserve of strength that allowed him to push forward and deliver a series of crushing blows to his opponent. To some of the onlookers, it seemed almost supernatural.

Accompanied by cheers of "Get up," from the crowd, Rocky attempted to pull himself back to his feet.

Apollo nearly made it to his feet, when his strength failed him and he ultimately slid back down the ropes.

The referee proclaimed Apollo to be knocked out, and Rocky as the new heavyweight champ.

Before embracing Mickey in victory, Rocky proclaimed triumphantly to TV cameras, "Yo, Adrian. I did it!"

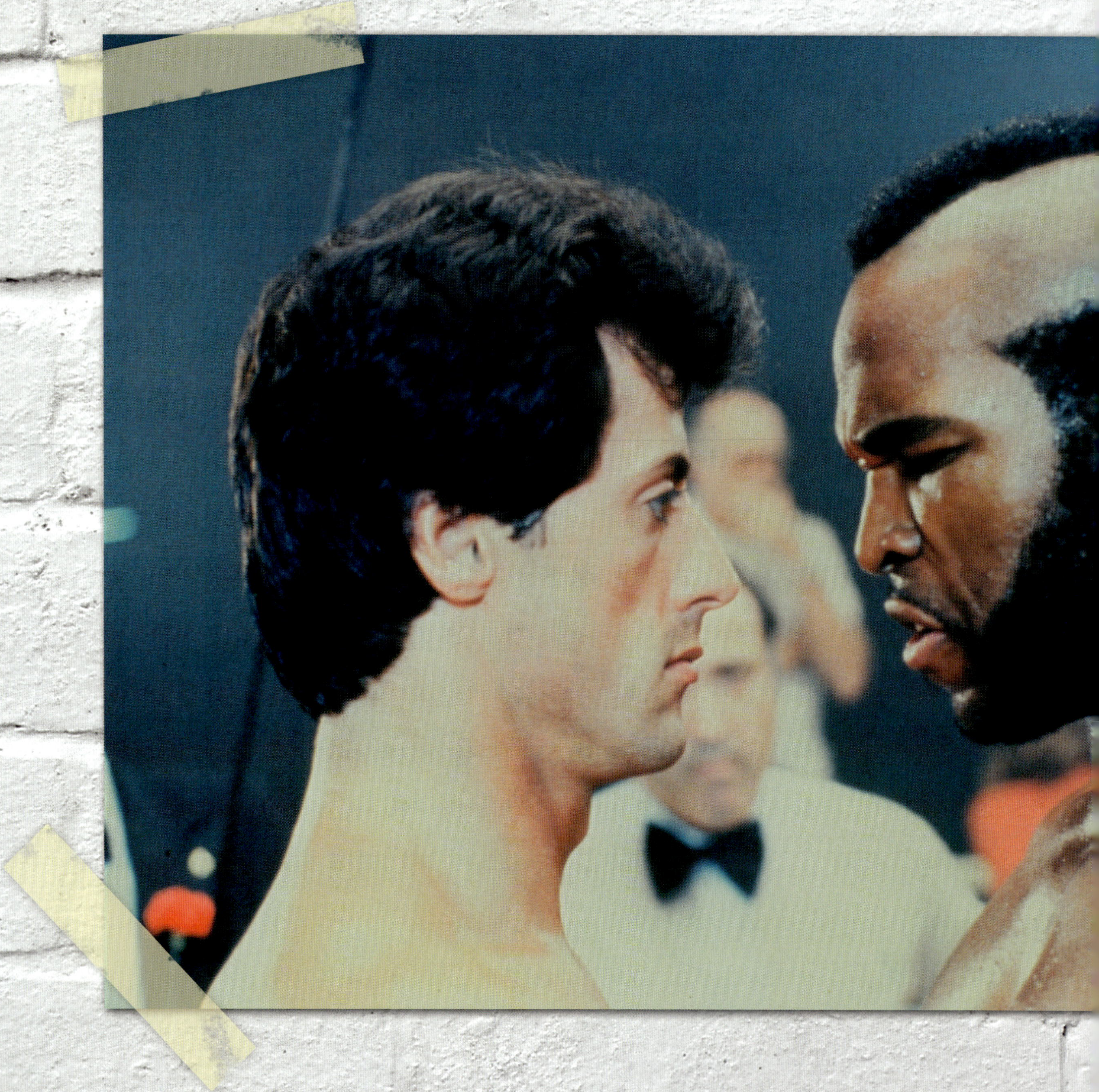

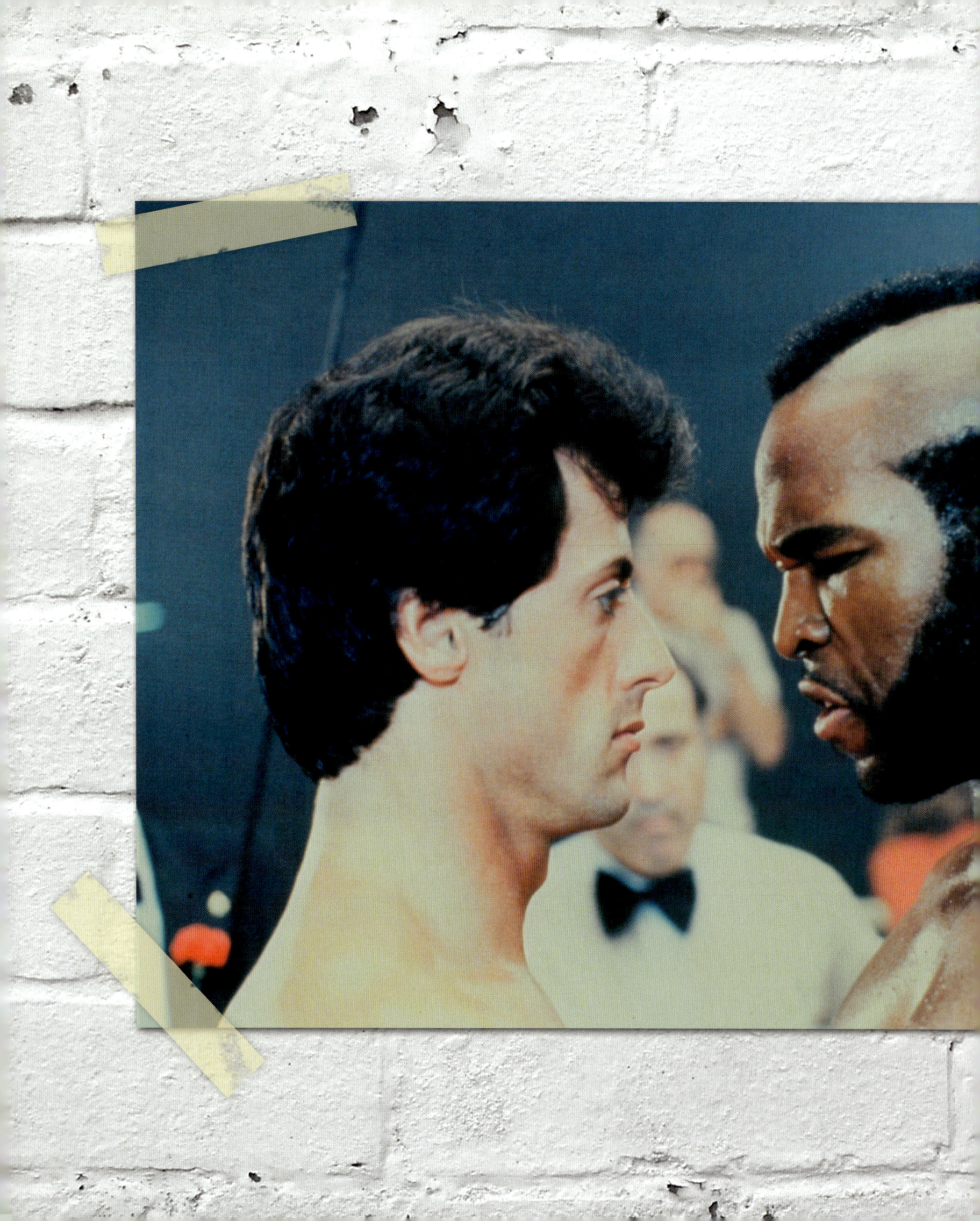

ROCKY III

WITH THE EXCEPTION of the original *Star Wars*, one would be hard-pressed to think of another Hollywood trilogy that scored in the way that *Rocky III* did. Under returning writer/director/star Sylvester Stallone's guiding hand, Rocky Balboa's third cinematic outing introduced the world to former bodyguard Mr. T as challenger, Clubber Lang. The character became an instant hit as the opponent audiences loved to hate, taking the title from Rocky, and—albeit unwittingly—bringing tragedy into the Italian Stallion's life. A tale of loss and triumph, *Rocky III* scores on a variety of levels, not least of which was the success of its theme song, "The Eye of the Tiger." The song, whose title was inspired by Apollo Creed's phrase meaning "killer edge," went on to become a worldwide hit and perhaps the best-known song ever to originate from a sports movie.

The Champ

"ROCKY CAN TAKE IT...SO CAN HIS TONY LAMAS." Footwear ad

PRIOR TO GETTING into the ring with Apollo Creed, for the second time neither Rocky nor Adrian had really given much thought to what a victory would mean to their lives. Rocky's main concern had been proving to the world that he wasn't just a no-name boxer who got lucky the first time out. For Adrian, it had been all about seeing her unwavering faith in her husband justified as he achieved his ambition. But their dreams had begun and ended with that moment of victory. As Rocky raised the champion's belt above his head in triumph, they both knew that that moment had arrived and their dreams had been fulfilled. Rocky's name was going to enter the history books as a Heavyweight Champion of the World. Now what? They were about to find out. Neither had any idea that their lives were about to change in ways that would ultimately eclipse the brief taste of wealth and status that they had enjoyed following the first fight. In fact, in many ways the victory over Apollo was to launch the Balboas onto a whole new stage of their lives.

Popular Champ
Rocky was truly a champion of the people, inspiring a rare degree of loyalty in his fans. He seemed such a regular guy, it was easy for fans to feel that each time he got into the ring, they were somehow getting in there with him.

The Good Life
In the three years following his close victory over Apollo Creed, Rocky's life became something of a whirlwind. His new ventures into the world of commercials were a huge success, and he found himself in demand as a spokesperson. His status in the public eye jumped dramatically with his many charitable efforts, and his image graced the covers of magazines everywhere. He even guest-starred on a number of television shows, including *The Muppet Show*. It had truly been an amazing journey. But with all this success, and the easy fights that Mickey arranged for him, Rocky was in danger of losing the hunger that had been his driving force.

Rocky engaged in no less than 10 title defenses, adding to his legion of fans with each victory.

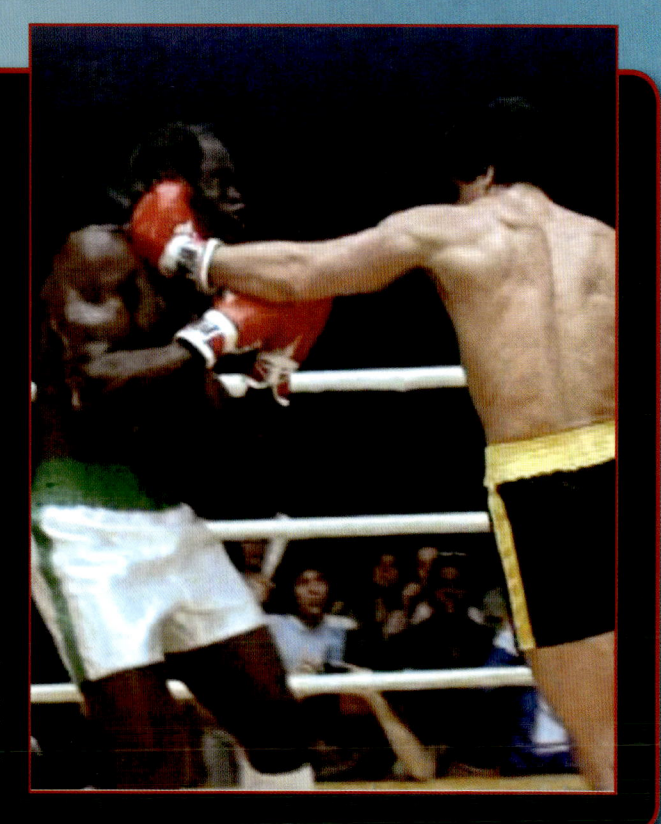

A New Contender

While Rocky was being swept along by his success and thoroughly enjoying the perks of fame he had little time to stop and take stock. Unbeknownst to him, a street fighter named Clubber Lang was quickly moving up through the boxing ranks. Lang was only too aware that Rocky's opponents were being hand-picked as easy prey. Tired of watching what he called a "paper champion" posing for photos ops, Lang had decided that this guy needed taking down—and that he would be the man to do it. Clubber Lang was going to take the title away from Rocky and be a true champion.

49

Thunderlips!

"THINK IT'S ALL FAKE, MEATBALL?" Thunderlips

ONE OF THE THINGS that most endeared Rocky to the public was his involvement with fundraising efforts for charity. When he agreed to take part in an exhibition match with wrestling champion Thunderlips, he was anticipating nothing more than a chance to provide the audience with a bit of fun and raise some money for a good cause. Thunderlips, however, was ready to inflict some serious pain on the boxer. It was nothing personal. His quarrel wasn't with Rocky, but with the media, who dismissed his sport as stage entertainment. This was his chance to show the world that a wrestling match could be every bit as exciting and unexpected as a bout between a couple of boxers.

ALL FOR CHARITY

Thunderlips was a giant of a man, nearly 7 feet tall and weighing in at 390lb. Rocky's reminder that the bout was for charity did nothing to make Mickey feel any better as they watched him approach the ring. "Nobody does this much for charity," he snapped. "Bob Hope would," offered Rocky.

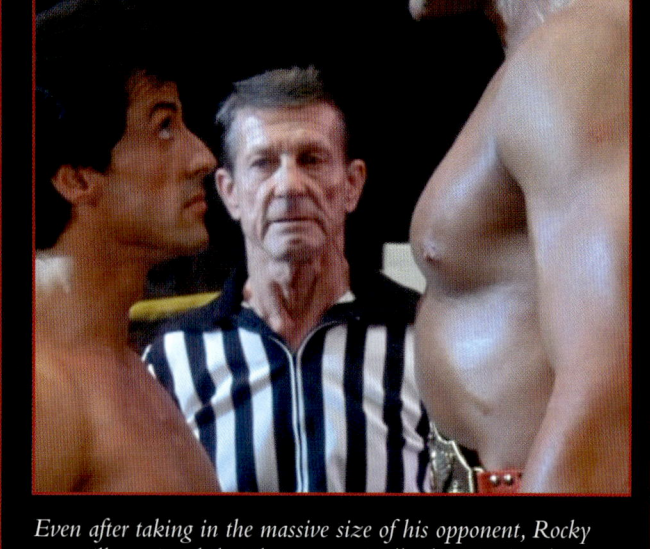

Even after taking in the massive size of his opponent, Rocky was still convinced that they were actually there to give the audience a good time. Thunderlips obviously had a different form of entertainment in mind…

Exhibition Battle

Before the fight, Rocky got his first clue that Thunderlips was taking it a little more seriously than he was. His suggestion that the two of them pose for a photo for the newspapers afterwards was met with a massive push from the wrestler. Nevertheless, Rocky continued to treat the bout as the exhibition he had expected. When the bell rang, he came forward, taking light jabs at Thunderlips and proposing that they should put on a bit of a show for the crowd, "First I'll chase you, then you chase me," he suggested. He was completely unprepared when the wrestler seemed suddenly to go insane, violently smashing Rocky over his knee, throwing him around the ring and hurling him outside the ropes.

Thunderlips shocked everyone by lifting Rocky over his head and carrying him around the ring.

Mickey experienced chest pains, caused by a serious heart problem he had been hiding from everyone.

Enraged, Rocky re-entered the ring and unleashed his fury, ultimately tossing Thunderlips out!

The match declared a draw, things calmed down and the Balboas and Thunderlips posed for that photo.

Clubber Lang

"HE AIN'T JUST ANOTHER FIGHTER, THIS GUY'S A WRECKIN' MACHINE"

IF THERE WERE a human equivalent to a wrecking machine, it would undoubtedly have taken the form of Clubber Lang. The boxer had managed to turn himself into a near-perfect machine of total destruction, capable of obliterating virtually anything that got in his way—and right now, Rocky Balboa was in his way. His ambition born out of what he felt was the adulation of a false champion, Clubber began training himself to become a boxer with one goal in mind. His strength, his energy, his ruthlessness were all focused on a single aim—to take the title from Rocky, a man he felt undeserving of wearing the gold heavyweight championship belt.

Angry Young Man

Perhaps the seeds of Clubber Lang's rage and hunger were sown in his tragic early life. He was abandoned by his parents at a young age and basically raised himself on the streets of Chicago, where he quickly learned that only the tough survive. In and out of trouble with the law, he spent almost as much time in juvenile detention and prison as he did walking the streets. It was while serving time in jail that Clubber took up boxing and, for the first time, discovered something positive into which he could channel his aggression. That seemingly limitless aggression was to earn him his nickname "The Southside Slugger." Solitary by nature, he was proud of the fact that he had never had any help in life from anyone—everything he achieved, he had achieved alone. Clubber didn't view Balboa as a hero, but as the perfect outlet for his rage.

Had anyone been looking, they would have seen Clubber Lang in the audience of many of Rocky's fights.

FIGHTING STYLE

Clubber Lang was a street brawler. Getting a man on his back wasn't enough for this fighter; he refused to be satisfied until he had smashed his opponent into unconsciousness, even if it meant throwing a referee aside to accomplish it. Lang's fists were destructive weapons and it didn't seem to matter what type of punches he threw—as long as they connected with an opponent the effect was guaranteed to be devastating. No fighter could go the distance with him; Clubber seemed more machine than man, operating without any sense of conscience or restraint.

> "YOU TELL BALBOA I'M COMIN' FOR HIM."
> CLUBBER LANG

No.1 Contender

While Rocky was settling into his role as champ and enjoying the lifestyle changes that went with it, Clubber entered the boxing world. With brutal determination he began fighting his way to the top, rapidly moving up the ranks. Clubber's success may have gone unnoticed by Rocky, but Mickey was only too aware of it. He was often in the crowd at Clubber's fights, taking stock of what he feared Rocky could one day be facing. That day seemed to be fast approaching when, after one particular bout, Lang caught sight of Mickey and began verbally abusing him, warning him that he would destroy Rocky.

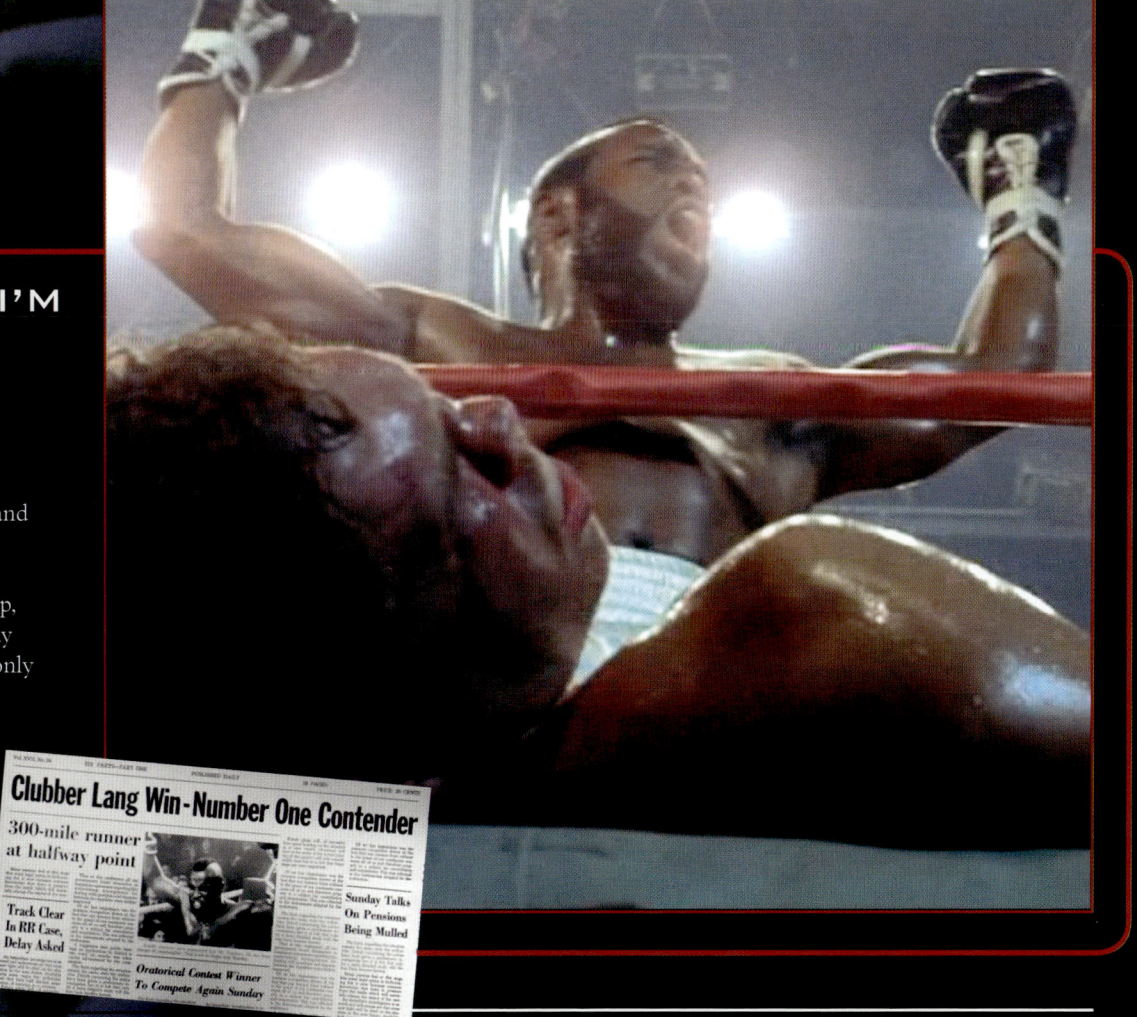

The Challenge

"DON'T GIVE THIS SUCKER A STATUE, GIVE HIM SOME GUTS!" CLUBBER LANG

OVER THE YEARS Rocky had become aware of the inspiration he was for people around the world, but the people of Philadelphia would always remain closest to his heart. So when the city unveiled a statue built in his honor, it brought home to him all over again not only how much he meant to those people, but how much they meant to him. Overwhelmed by his feelings for the people and the city itself, Rocky wanted them to know his decision about the next stage of his life before anyone else did. That's why he chose that moment to make the announcement that he felt the time was right for him to step down and retire. By quitting while at the top, he would always remain in the people's memories as their hero—the undefeated champion. Unfortunately it was an idea that didn't sit well with boxer Clubber Lang, as Lang made very clear to those gathered around them.

ON A PEDESTAL

Gazing at the 9ft-tall bronze statue, Rocky was struck by how larger-than-life his image had become. In a way, being celebrated as a hero like this made him feel uncomfortable. Yet it also made him feel obligated to live up to people's perceptions of him—to act with dignity and be the very best he could.

CLUBBER BUTTS IN

Clubber pushed his way to the front of the crowd, announcing himself as the number one contender and loudly accusing Rocky of retiring to avoid a real title challenger. When Rocky refused to take the bait, Clubber turned his attention to Adrian, teasing her about how she probably dreamed of being with "a real man." That did it—at last Rocky snapped, angrily accepting Lang's challenge there and then.

The Truth At Last

Mickey's public statement that Clubber would get no shot at the title was surprising enough, but his abrupt departure from the statue ceremony was even more of a shock. It wasn't until later that Rocky found out the reason: Mickey felt that there was no way he could win against this particular fighter. For the first time he learned the painful truth: all his previous title defenses had been "hand-picked" to present him with easy victories. Clubber, on the other hand, was a hungry fighter and that hunger gave him the kind of edge that Rocky had lost a long time ago. "You ain't been hungry since you won that belt," Mickey admitted.

The First Fight

"YOU MADE ME WAIT TOO LONG, BALBOA!" Clubber Lang

MAYBE IT WAS DENIAL or maybe it was over-confidence, but at the outset Rocky wasn't nearly as concerned about the fight with Clubber Lang as Mickey was. Even after hearing the truth from Mickey, he only half believed that Lang was the "wrecking machine" that his trainer described. Having succeeded in talking Mickey—against his better judgement—into sticking with him for "just one more fight," Rocky launched himself into a training program that seemed mainly geared toward publicity. Mickey's continued warnings seemed to have no effect, and even as the fighters were getting ready to enter the ring, Rocky genuinely didn't seem worried.

TRAINING CONTRAST
While training, Rocky played to the public and the camera, while Clubber Lang undertook a private, intensely grueling route. Ironically, Rocky had become victim of the same kind of complacency that Apollo Creed had exhibited prior to their first fight.

TUNNEL TUSSLE
A verbal confrontation between Rocky and Clubber would have turned physical if not for their respective teams. The fighters were separated, but in the chaos Mickey suffered massive chest pains after an accidental push by Clubber. Shocked and concerned, Rocky suggested they needed to cancel the fight, but Mick insisted he get out there and win.

"DEAD MEAT..." Clubber

Round 1
In the seconds leading up to the first round, Rocky was consumed with thoughts of Mickey. He could barely keep his mind on the task that was before him. Clubber Lang had become a mere nuisance, a distraction from what was really important. Rocky just wanted to get this fight over as quickly as possible and rejoin his mentor and friend. With the sound of the bell, he moved aggressively to the center of the ring and launched an all-out attack against Lang. Body blows, jabs—Rocky put everything he had behind them and all of them connected with their target. But why, he remembered thinking before he lost all cognizant thought, wasn't this man falling? The answer became obvious almost immediately when Clubber delivered a devastating blow that instantly stunned him. This was followed by another, then another, then still more, and with horror Rocky realized that he had no defense against this man.

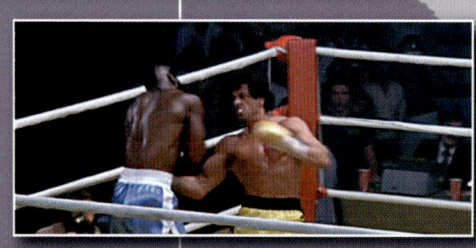

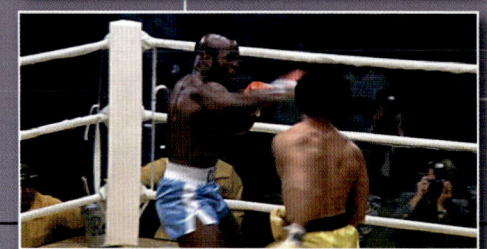

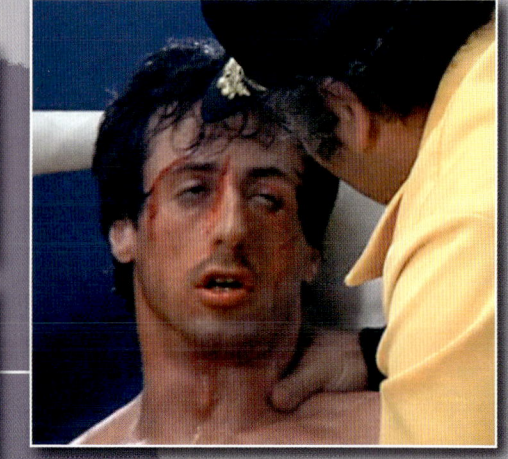

Round 2

With the second round bell, Rocky took the offensive again, coming out swinging, but his punch had no power and did nothing to halt Clubber Lang's assault. Now firmly in control, Lang didn't hesitate to unleash his full fury. The attack was merciless, and seconds later Rocky collapsed to the ground, his figure appearing tiny and insignificant in the center of the Italian Stallion logo that adorned the canvas. He knew that he was supposed to get up, but found it impossible to do so. He felt as if the heart had gone out of him. At that moment, Rocky's reign as champion was over.

2

As he counts Rocky out, the referee sees the boxer make no attempt to rise.

His thoughts elsewhere, Rocky lies motionless on the canvas, beaten in spirit as much as in body.

"I LOVE YOU, KID." MICKEY

The Aftermath

"I'M A LIAR, AND BECAUSE OF IT MICKEY'S DEAD." Rocky

DISORIENTED AND ON the verge of collapse, Rocky made his way to the locker room, ignoring the roar from the crowd as the new champion was ushered in. For him, the crowd didn't matter. Neither did the beating he had taken. The only thing that mattered, and the only thing keeping him on his feet, was the need to get back to Mickey; to talk to him and tell him that everything was going to be alright. Barely able to see, Mick dimly recognized the hooded figure before him as Rocky, but could only gasp out a few words, asking Rocky if it was over. Rocky replied that it was; finished with a knockout in the second round. Believing this to mean that Rocky had somehow prevailed over Clubber Lang despite the odds, the older man smiled and managed a raspy, "I love you, kid" before he slipped away. Collapsing to his knees, Rocky, who had not shed a single tear during his fight with Lang or for the loss of the heavyweight title, let out a wail of agony, his sobs echoing throughout the locker room. Mickey, the only father that Rocky had ever really known, was gone, and in that moment he felt very much alone.

Mickey's Funeral

During the service for Mickey, Rocky looked at Adrian and Paulie and realized that the three of them had come to represent Mickey's family. He reflected on his confrontation with Mickey all those years ago, how they almost didn't team up, and how tragic that would have been. Rocky probably would never have beaten Apollo and Mickey would have undoubtedly died alone.

Rocky couldn't shake his feelings of guilt over Mickey's death, and his insecurities about his own future.

It was near-impossible for Rocky to reconcile his current life with the larger-than-life perception of it.

THE RETURN OF APOLLO

Rocky was startled when Apollo Creed turned up at Mickey's now-deserted gym one night. Apollo had come with an extraordinary proposition. Admitting that since his retirement things had gotten too quiet for him, he offered to be Rocky's new manager. He was convinced he could help him to rediscover the "eye of the tiger" and reclaim the title from Lang.

Starting Over

"THERE IS NO TOMORROW... THERE IS NO TOMORROW!" APOLLO

INITIALLY, ROCKY WAS FIRED UP by Apollo's offer to train him for a rematch with Clubber Lang. Filled with enthusiasm, he whole-heartedly agreed to re-locate to Los Angeles so that Apollo could get back to his roots. If successful, they would essentially be regaining the title together—Rocky in reality and Apollo in spirit. But no sooner had they begun than Rocky came face to face with something he never experienced before—a loss of confidence. It ate away at him, destroying his focus and preventing him from putting his heart into his training. He was haunted not only by feelings of guilt over Mickey's death, but by the memory of all those easy fights Mickey had arranged for him. Had he gone all those years thinking he was better than he was? Rocky could barely acknowledge that fear to himself, let alone voice it to anyone else. Instead, he withdrew, becoming less and less cooperative. It all culminated with Apollo exploding, demanding an explanation and, finally, admitting defeat. As far as he was concerned, it was over.

When the media mocked Rocky for agreeing to a rematch with Clubber Lang, Apollo promised him that after the fight they'd owe him an apology.

Creed pushed Rocky harder and harder, trying to rediscover that killer edge he knew was buried somewhere deep inside the ex-champ. But Rocky failed to respond. The most he could offer was that he would try harder "tomorrow."

New Tricks

Could a boxer who had been accustomed to training a certain way for his entire professional career completely relearn his craft? Apollo had warned Rocky that he was going to have to forget everything that he had ever been taught and get back to basics. But perhaps he hadn't really appreciated how hard that was going to be (he was often overheard mumbling, "Mick never had me do this.") Before long Rocky began to feel that it was an impossible task, and that thought rapidly became overwhelming, almost paralyzing. Paulie's negative comments over the situation did nothing to help, but only served to reinforce the doubts already filling Rocky's mind.

Apollo's methods were supposed to help Rocky to build speed, so that he could end the fight before running "out of steam," but Rocky was unable to motivate himself.

A crisis of confidence: shortly before everything seemed to implode during training, Rocky quite literally faced himself in the mirror, wrestling with his doubts.

TOUGH LOVE

Adrian confronted Rocky on the beach, demanding to know what was going on. Unable to hide the truth any longer, he finally admitted that for the first time in his life he was afraid, and that he no longer believed in himself. Sensing that this was a make or break moment for Rocky, Adrian didn't hold back. For the first time, she raised her voice to her husband. Losing to Lang again, she told him, would be something he could live with. Quitting out of fear, on the other hand, would haunt him for the rest of his life.

> "HOW DID YOU GET SO TOUGH?"
> ROCKY
>
> "I LIVE WITH A FIGHTER."
> ADRIAN

Adrian's words hit home to Rocky. With her love and support he felt like he could achieve almost anything.

Confidence restored, Rocky accepted Apollo's challenge for a race along the beach. Unlike in earlier races he was victorious, and Apollo knew they had turned a corner.

With Adrian's words still ringing in his head, Rocky threw himself completely into the task at hand, transforming himself into a very different kind of fighter. At last he was living up to Apollo's expectations. He had finally achieved the prized "eye of the tiger."

Second Chance

"GONNA BUST YOU UP." Clubber Lang
"GO FOR IT." Rocky

Entering the ring, Clubber expected nothing less than a quick victory over Rocky, proving once again to the world that the man they had called a champion was nothing more than a joke. But Rocky was not the same man he had been when he first encountered the current champ. His confidence in himself was now fully restored, and his appetite sharpened. Furthermore, thanks to Adrian, he had something even more important—the instinctive knowledge that even if he did not walk out of this bout the winner, it wouldn't matter because he had overcome so many obstacles. If he was going out, he would go out the way he lived most of his life: fighting.

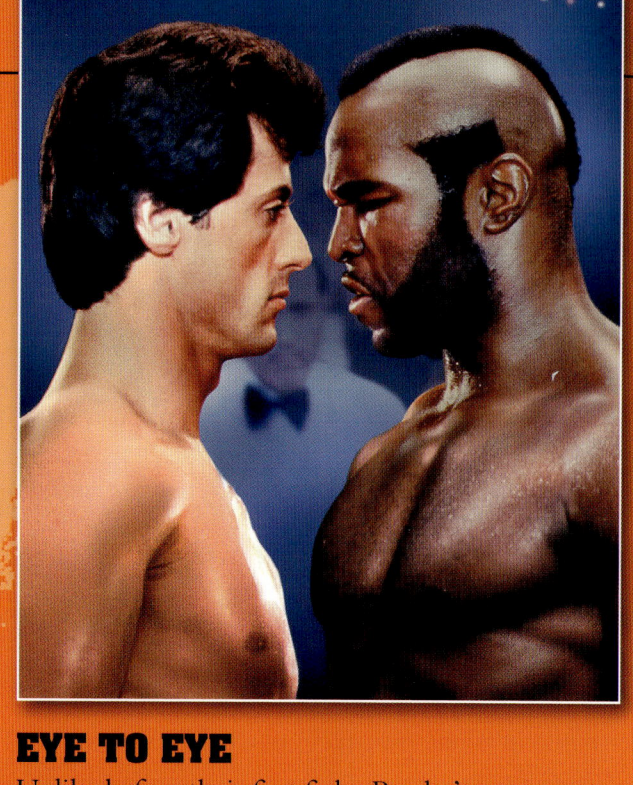

EYE TO EYE
Unlike before their first fight, Rocky's gaze never wavered from Clubber's. No matter how hard the champ tried, he could not make Rocky flinch. Judging by his attitude heading to his corner, this obviously had a psychological effect on Clubber.

Round 1
With the sound of the bell, Rocky sprang into action, surprising the crowd by displaying an agility and lightness of foot unlike anything he had shown before. In fact he was dancing around the ring exactly like Apollo Creed used to, flicking out one jab after another. Almost all of these blows found their target on Clubber Lang, who was enraged to find himself quickly disoriented by Rocky's new, and completely unexpected style of fighting. Instead of relying on raw power, Rocky would move in, deliver a series of blows, and then dance away, evading just about everything that Clubber threw his way. By the time the first round—which Rocky won decisively—was over, a furiously screaming Clubber had to be dragged back into his corner by his team, unable to accept what had happened. "I don't think Lang knew what hit him," remarked a commentator at the ringside.

Round 2
Initially, the second series of exchanges seemed to mirror that of the first, but then Clubber took an opportunity to deliver one of his killer blows to Rocky. This was followed by another and then a third. Rocky got a few punches in, but was repeatedly slammed by Clubber. He went down once and then a second time as Clubber continued to unleash ferocious punches. Amazingly, though, at the end of the round, Rocky had enought left to actually begin taunting his opponent, proclaiming that his mother hit harder than that. In disbelief, Clubber referred to him as a "stupid fool," to which Rocky retorted, "At least I ain't breathing heavy." Surprised to see Rocky verbally winding up his opponent Apollo demanded an explanation, but Rocky simply dismissed it as "strategy."

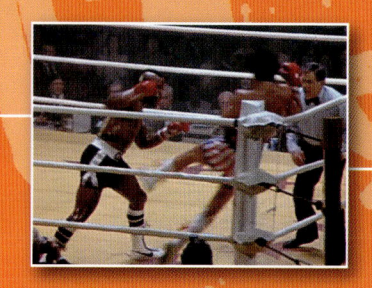

"I KNOW WHAT I'M DOING. IT'S STRATEGY." Rocky

Round 3

Thinking he had gained the upper hand, Clubber moved into round three determined to crush Rocky, ignoring pleas from his camp not to go toe-to-toe with him. He came out and began firing off staggering body blows, but Rocky simply absorbed them, watching the champion getting more and more exhausted as he punched himself out. Then, sensing his moment, Rocky suddenly turned the tables, began evading punches and exploded with an unbelievable series of jabs, body blows and punches to the head. Clubber was completely off balance and, in turn, defenseless. Blow after blow found its mark. He slowed, staggered and, finally, went down to the canvas. He lay there, shaking his head; attempting to figure out exactly how to get back up on his feet, but ultimately failing to do so. The referee counted him out, and Rocky was declared Heavyweight Champion of the World once again. Now it was time for Apollo to call in his "favor."

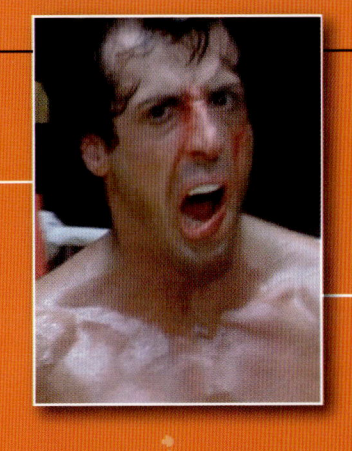

"HE'S GETTING KILLED OUT THERE." Apollo

"NO, HE'S GETTING MAD!" Paulie

Rocky's new style of boxing combines lightness of foot with sheer power.

Having punched himself out, Clubber is too exhausted to dodge Rocky's blows.

Clubber finds himself in an unfamiliar position—sprawled on the canvas.

REBIRTH OF A CHAMPION

When Rocky reclaimed the heavyweight title from Clubber Lang, the ring announcer proclaimed that his victory had shocked the world. In retrospect, maybe it shouldn't have been such a shock. By that time the potential of Rocky to raise his game should never have been in question. Somehow he had always managed to defy the odds, to do the unexpected and prove himself victorious—whether that was going the distance with Apollo Creed, uniting with his adversary in a boxer/trainer partnership, or taking on and defeating Lang. This was a man with a truly extraordinary spirit.

The Favor

"THIS IS EXTREMELY CRAZY, APOLLO."
Rocky

WHEN APOLLO APPROACHED ROCKY that night in Mickey's gym offering to train him for a rematch with Lang, he brought with him an agenda. That agenda took the form of a major favor that he wanted regardless of whether Rocky won or lost the fight. Creed was to remind Rocky of this favor at various times during their training, but he kept its nature a secret until the right moment. At last, when the title was safely back in Rocky's hands, that moment came. Then, Apollo explained that Rocky beating him by just one second in their last fight was something that he had never come to terms with. It was, he told Rocky, something that "a man of my intelligence can't handle." Rocky laughed at that; Apollo had previously assured him that he'd learned to live with the defeat and he had believed it. Now he realized that had obviously been a lie. With Clubber defeated, it was time for Apollo to call Rocky in on that favor: he wanted the two of them to step between the ropes and fight it out to determine once and for all who was the better fighter. Apollo didn't want any form of media and he didn't want an audience of any kind—for a showman like him, shocking in itself. All he wanted was for the two of them to get into the ring, with just one of them walking out.

Foes Become Friends

In the beginning, Apollo had dismissed Rocky as something of a joke while Rocky viewed him with awe. In the ring the two fighters had become fierce adversaries while developing a deep mutual respect and now, having united against Clubber Lang, that repect had become true friendship.

When asked when he'd come up with this idea, Apollo admitted it was right after their rematch.

The fact that there was a private rematch between Rocky and Apollo was never revealed to anyone. The results of that rematch were to forever to remain a secret between the two men.

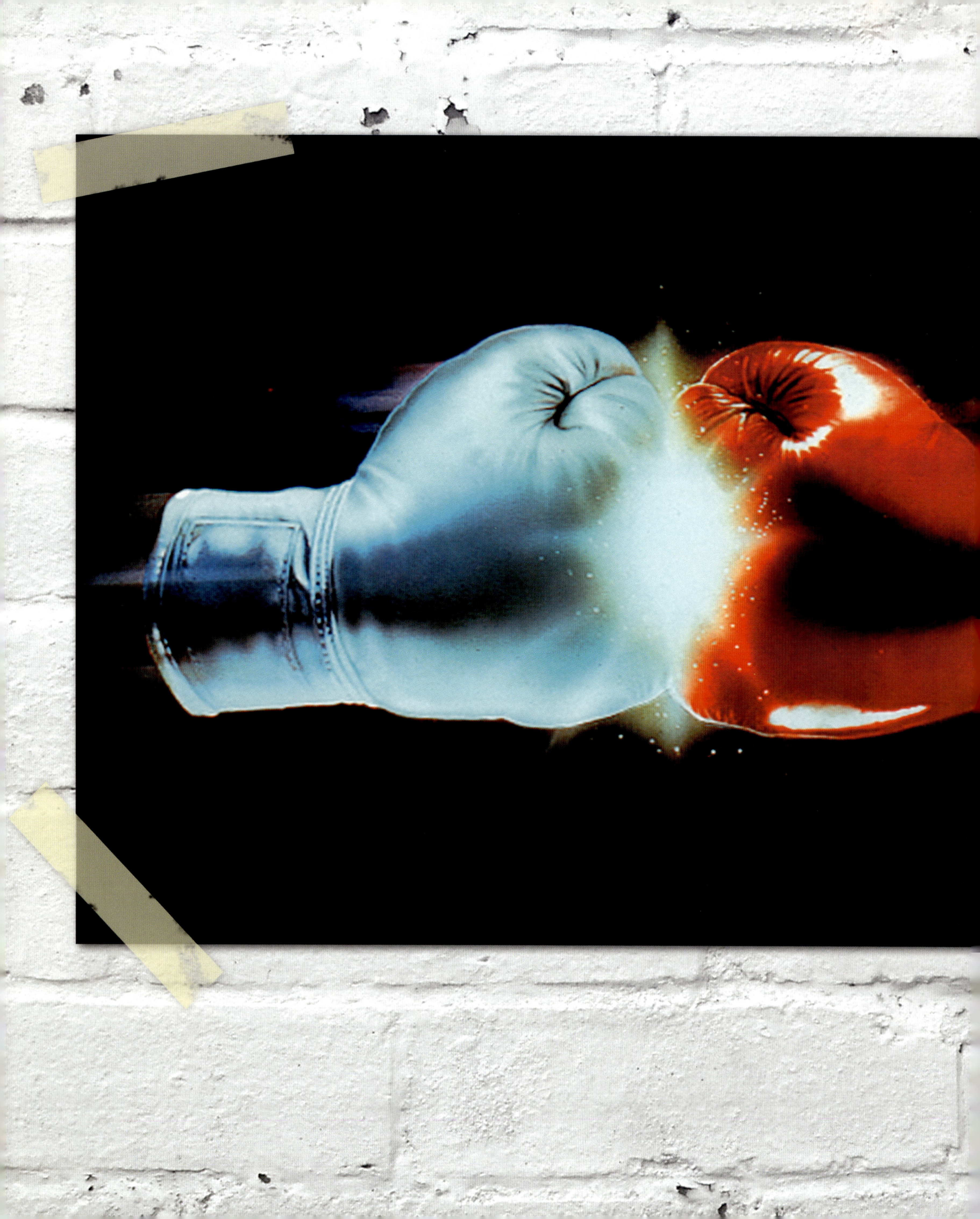

ROCKY IV

Having come back to defeat Clubber Lang in their rematch, Rocky Balboa had done the seemingly impossible. It was a feat mirrored by his creator, Sylvester Stallone. To have created a successful sequel to Rocky was one thing, but to have pulled that feat off a second time with *Rocky III* was simply unbelievable. That film had not only ended up grossing more than either of its predecessors, but had been a critical hit as well. It was more or less inevitable that there was going to have to be a *Rocky IV*. The challenge, of course, was finding a fresh slant—one that wouldn't make the story feel like more of the same. Stallone needed to find a new kind of opponent for Rocky. What he came up with was a stroke of genius. It was the mid 1980s, and the Cold War between America and Russia was at an all-time high, and the two countries were viewed as the reigning superpowers of the world. Stallone decided that Rocky should battle his Soviet equivalent and fighting machine Ivan Drago was born. Thus America and Russia got to slug it out—allegorically—in the ring in a movie that truly captured the spirit of the time.

East vs. West

"THIS IS ABOUT US AGAINST THEM" APOLLO CREED

BEFORE HIS REMATCH with Clubber Lang, Rocky had felt that if he could only win this one, there would be nothing left to prove. Now, having prevailed over such incredible odds, he found himself feeling completely reinvigorated. His appetite for the game was as sharp as ever, and he decided to stay in boxing a little longer. This was a golden time for Rocky; back to his peak as a fighter, secure in his friendship with Apollo, and enjoying a happy family life with Adrian, Rocky Jr., and Paulie. There was no way he could have foreseen that a force from the Soviet Union was about to hit America—one that would change the life of him and his loved ones forever.

Paulie had hoped for a sports car for his birthday, so he was disappointed when Rocky and Adrian gave him a six-foot robot. He later changed his mind when he realized he would never again have to fetch his own beer.

Enter the Drago

The arrival of Russian boxer Ivan Drago and his entourage of handlers—some of them official agents of the Soviet government—created something of a circus atmosphere. The press desperately tried to get an interview or, at the very least, further information on why they had come to America. They didn't have to wait long for an answer. The Soviets were were there to demonstrate to the West their progress in the area of boxing, and were hoping to arrange an exhibition match on American soil.

"We hope to set up an exibition match with your champion, Rocky Balboa."

APOLLO TUNES IN

Retirement was painful for Apollo. Training Rocky for his fight with Clubber had proven as rejuvenating to him as it had for the champ, and in its aftermath he was beginning to feel adrift; a man without a purpose. So his attention was instantly drawn to the television screen when he heard the news that Russia had decided to throw its hat into the ring; the boxing ring. At that moment Apollo, a true patriot, knew exactly what he had to do.

As he watched the Russians' press conference on television, Apollo felt rage swelling up within him. What he saw was the Soviet propaganda machine at work.

Stand By Me

Arriving at Rocky and Adrian's home, Apollo lost no time in expressing his desire that he, not Rocky, should be the one to participate in the exhibition bout with Drago. But when he asked if he could count on Rocky's support, Rocky was reluctant. The fact was Apollo hadn't been in the ring for years, and although Rocky could see how much this fight meant to his friend, he tried to dissuade him as tactfully as he could.

Apollo brushed aside Rocky's concerns. "I'm asking you to stand in my corner one more time," he said.

Before leaving Rocky and Apollo to talk amongst themselves, Adrian reminded them both that neither had anything left to prove to anyone.

Finally, loyalty won out over caution, and Rocky agreed to give Creed his wholehearted support.

Ivan Drago

"WHATEVER HE HITS, HE DESTROYS!" NIKOLI KOLOFF

KEPT IN ISOLATION and living a life that consisted of little else than training as a boxer, Ivan Drago had begun to lose his sense of self. He felt as though he were becoming more of a machine than a man, a machine designed with only one goal in mind—to prove Russia's supremacy in the ring. Plucked from the ranks of the Soviet army, he had been told that he would become a national symbol, a hero to the people, and a badge of honor to his homeland. Drago hadn't been interested in any of that. But he had been interested—very interested—in the opportunity to develop as a boxer and prove himself a greater champion than the man who had inspired him to take up the sport in the first place, Rocky Balboa. Politics was not Drago's game; he would leave that to others. Proving his craft in the boxing ring was everything. When he fought, he would fight not for Russia, but for himself.

Ludmilla

Ludmilla Vobet Drago's marriage to Ivan had not been built on love, but on her duty to her country. She had been assigned to Ivan when it became obvious that she had caught his attention, and she was more or less instructed to cut short the courtship period so that he would not be distracted from the task at hand. Her sole purpose was to make him feel good about himself, and to reinforce how important all of this was not only for them as a couple, but for the Soviet Union itself. Clearly, she had done her job extremely well. It wasn't the most romantic of beginnings, but some time prior to their first trip to America, the statuesque blonde had realized that she was beginning to have genuine feelings for her husband. Whether or not this had more to do with his status and the effect that success in America would have on their lives back home was something that she didn't permit herself to spend too much time thinking about.

In the Spotlight

Generally speaking, training in Russia was done in secret, the press only having access to what the government wanted them to see. So to be in America where the reporters were virtually everywhere they went, whether they wanted them there or not, was a bit overwhelming for both Ivan and Ludmilla. The attention they'd gotten since arriving in the United States was far more than either had expected, though one would be hard-pressed to recognize a look of surprise—or any emotion for that matter—on Drago's face. But they and their team, particularly Nicoli Koloff, the Russian spokesman, were quick to turn this press intrusion to their advantage. Ludmilla in particular charmed the press corp with her ice-cool beauty and fluent command of English.

The Russians were happy to exploit any PR value they could in demonstrating Drago's superior hitting ability as well as the hi-tech equipment that he used to train on.

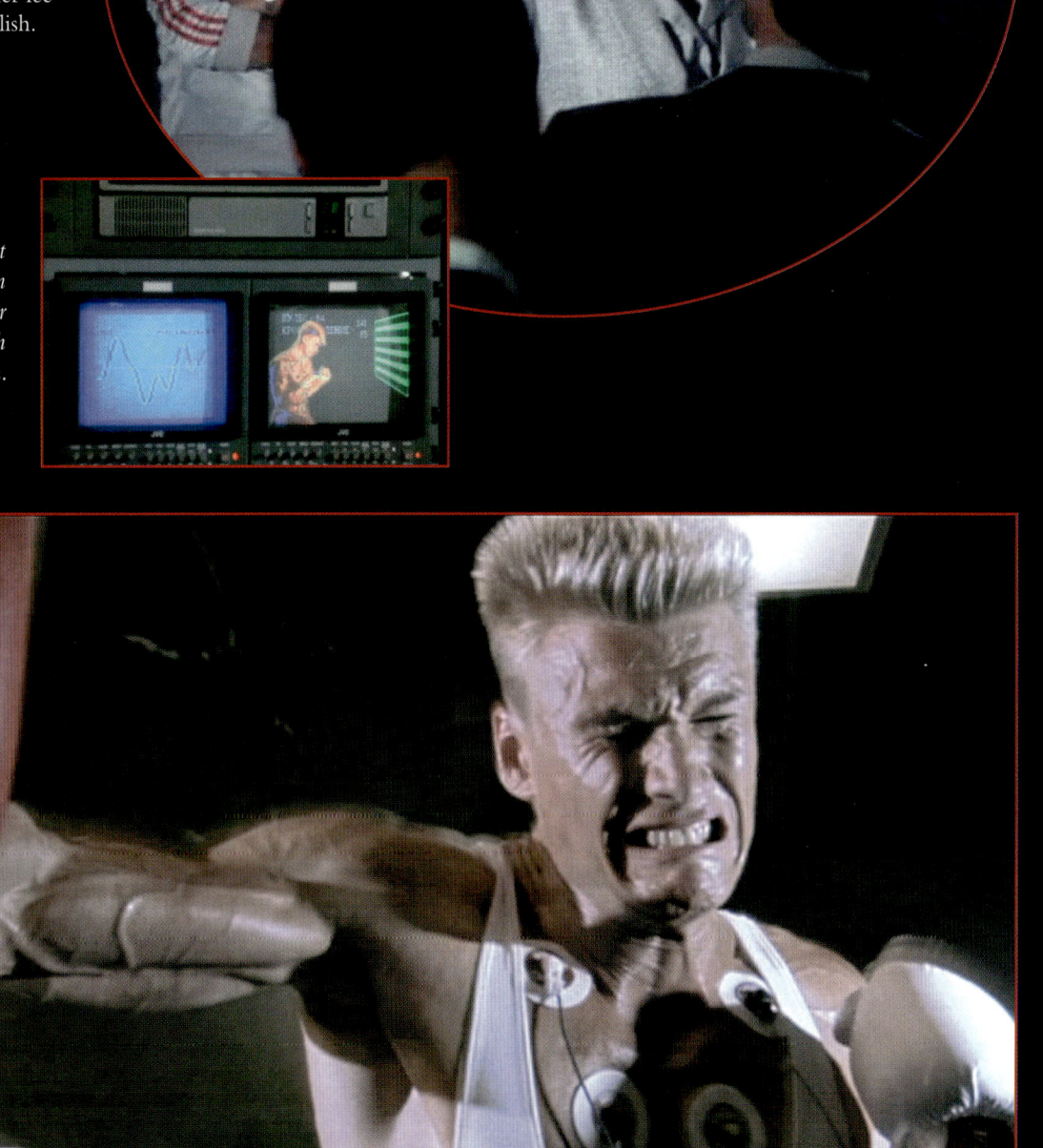

Asked whether Drago's seemingly impossible strength was natural or enhanced by the use of steroids, Ludmilla replied "like your Popeye, he ate his spinach."

Tension Mounts

The press conference prior to the fight began cordially enough, with Apollo offering a few good-natured jabs at Drago and cracking wise to the press. Things took a nosedive, however, when Ludmilla's compliment that Apollo was very well respected in Russia ended with the statement, "It should be a good victory." To Apollo, that sounded like sheer arrogance.

Creed's outrage at the suggestion that Drago would beat him was met by Ludmilla's cool "We didn't come here to lose."

When Koloff dismissed Apollo as "too old," and Apollo called him "Comrade Bigmouth," all pretense of civility vanished.

Press Conference

"I'VE RETIRED MORE MEN THAN SOCIAL SECURITY." APOLLO CREED

UP UNTIL THE MOMENT when it all descended into chaos, Drago had sat through the press conference observing everything with barely hidden contempt. All this talking, talking, talking seemed so pointless to him—he would rather have been training. The lure of the gym tugged at him as it so often did; somehow he felt that if he wasn't there, he was doing something wrong. Apollo, on the other hand, was back in his element for the first time in what seemed like forever. As he sat there insulting the challenger and bantering with the reporters, he felt himself reconnecting with the media in a way he hadn't been able to for several years. He had allowed himself to settle into being a mere observer or a commentator—but now he was back at the center of a media firestorm, and he loved it. In fact he *needed* it to feel truly alive. It was as though the clock was somehow turned backwards, and he was the Apollo Creed of old again.

"We'll finish this in the ring"

Things seemed to be spiralling out of control, and Drago and Apollo looked as if they were about to come to blows. Seconds later, Apollo was on his feet warning the much taller Russian that they would finish this in the ring, his bravado for just a moment making everyone forget the sheer size of his opponent. That Creed had been playing it to the press was evident when, as soon as they were out of the Russians' earshot, he asked Rocky what he thought of his performance.

After the press conference, Apollo asked Rocky for reassurance that his performance had been OK.

All-American Show

"YOU MUST FIND OUT WHO YOU ARE" JAMES BROWN

APOLLO CREED, showman extraordinaire, was back! Determined to make this more than just a boxing match, he resolved to dazzle the gathered Las Vegas crowd with a show they would never forget. He elected to embrace Hollywood excess (and take a cheeky shot at the Russians) by having James Brown perform his song "Living in America." The stage turned boxing ring was alive with dancers and extravagant set pieces, and Apollo surveyed the incredible scene with undisguised relish. Just before the fight he confessed to Rocky that he felt reborn. He hadn't felt this good since '76, and in fact by coming out dressed as Uncle Sam, wearing his red, white, and blue trunks as he had done on that day, he almost felt as if he were recreating that moment. The old connection he had felt with the crowd was still there, stronger than ever. It was a sensation both familiar and strangely new; as though the real Apollo had returned after a long time away.

Before the fight, Drago was led to an underground boxing ring. After words of encouragement from his wife and advisors, the roof opened and the ring began to rise.

Drago's View

Throughout his life, Drago had heard a lot about the freedom enjoyed by Americans, but he couldn't wrap his mind around all he had seen since first arriving in the country. People here seemed to do and say whatever they pleased, and the effect was frequently one of chaos. As he stood in the ring waiting for the fight to begin, Drago was about to experience that chaos magnified a thousand times—and for the first time up close. He was about to find himself at the center of a full-scale, all-American extravaganza!

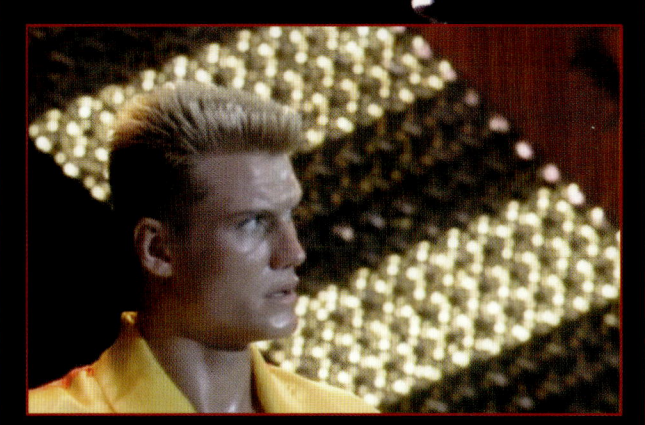

With confusion showing on his face, Drago felt like an animal on display in the zoo. He wondered how the audience would react to seeing this animal unleashed.

Lowered down from an elevated platform, Apollo began to toy playfully with Drago as the crowd roared its approval.

When Ludmilla approached Apollo's wife with an offer of friendship, it was, in reality, nothing more than a photo opportunity. She had obviously learned to play the game.

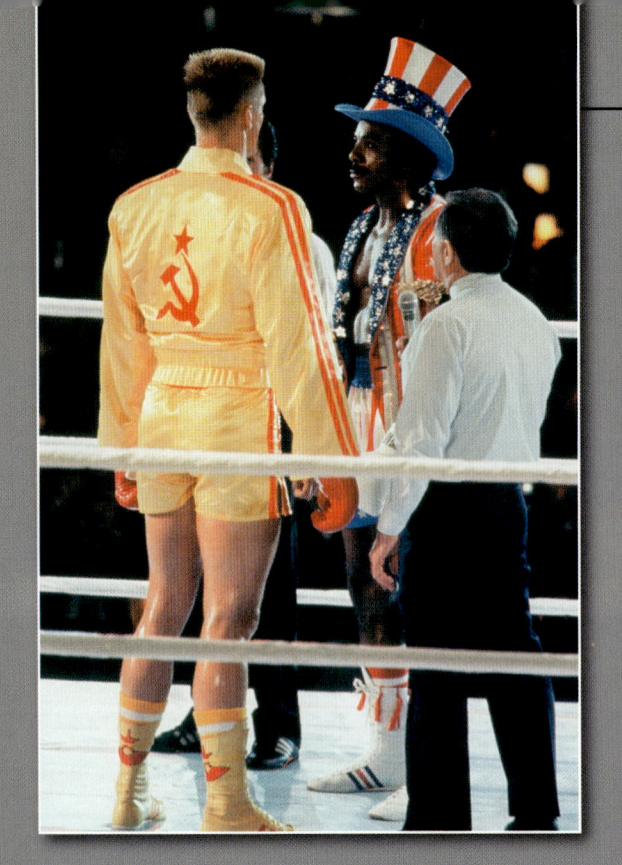

Apollo's Last Fight

"IF HE DIES, HE DIES" DRAGO

AS THE MUSIC FADED AWAY and the dancers left the stage, the two fighters were brought to the center of the ring for instructions from the referee. Watching the grim-faced Russian as he towered over Apollo, Rocky felt his old fears resurfacing. He was worried that Apollo, who hadn't been in the ring for so long, had not taken the fight seriously enough. Although it was only supposed to be an exhibition match, Rocky instinctively felt that to Drago and his people it was much more important. Why couldn't Apollo see the same thing? And the reassuring wink Apollo threw his way during the instructions was anything but comforting.

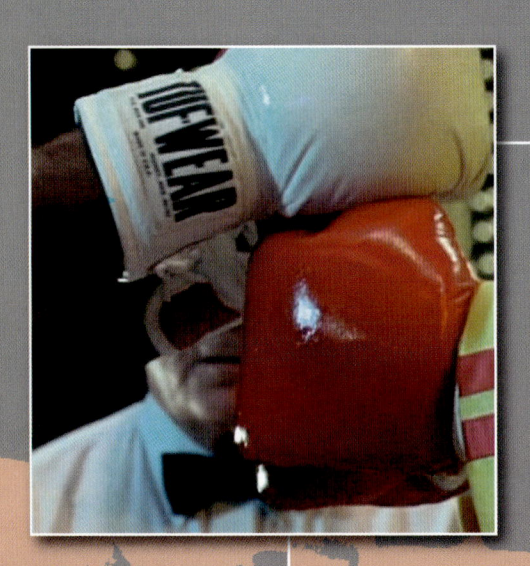

Round 1

Both fighters moved to the center of the ring. Apollo began confidently, dancing around in his trademark style, flicking out jabs followed by combinations. But although some of the blows were connecting with Drago, it quickly became apparent that they weren't really having much impact. In fact, apart from occasionally moving his head from side to side to avoid them, Drago didn't at first seem to be doing much at all. He practically stood in one place, his right arm cocked, while it was left to Apollo to do all the work. And then, suddenly, all hell broke loose when Drago delivered a devastating punch. Followed by another, and then another. Apollo had no defense against the onslaught. Bloodied almost immediately, he was soon staggering and on the point of collapse. The bell rang, saving him from going down, but even then Drago kept up his assault. He was like a punching machine. Back in the corner, Rocky wanted the fight stopped immediately. "He's killing you!" he warned Apollo. But Creed refused, demanding to see it through to the end.

"DON'T STOP THE FIGHT... NO MATTER WHAT!" APOLLO

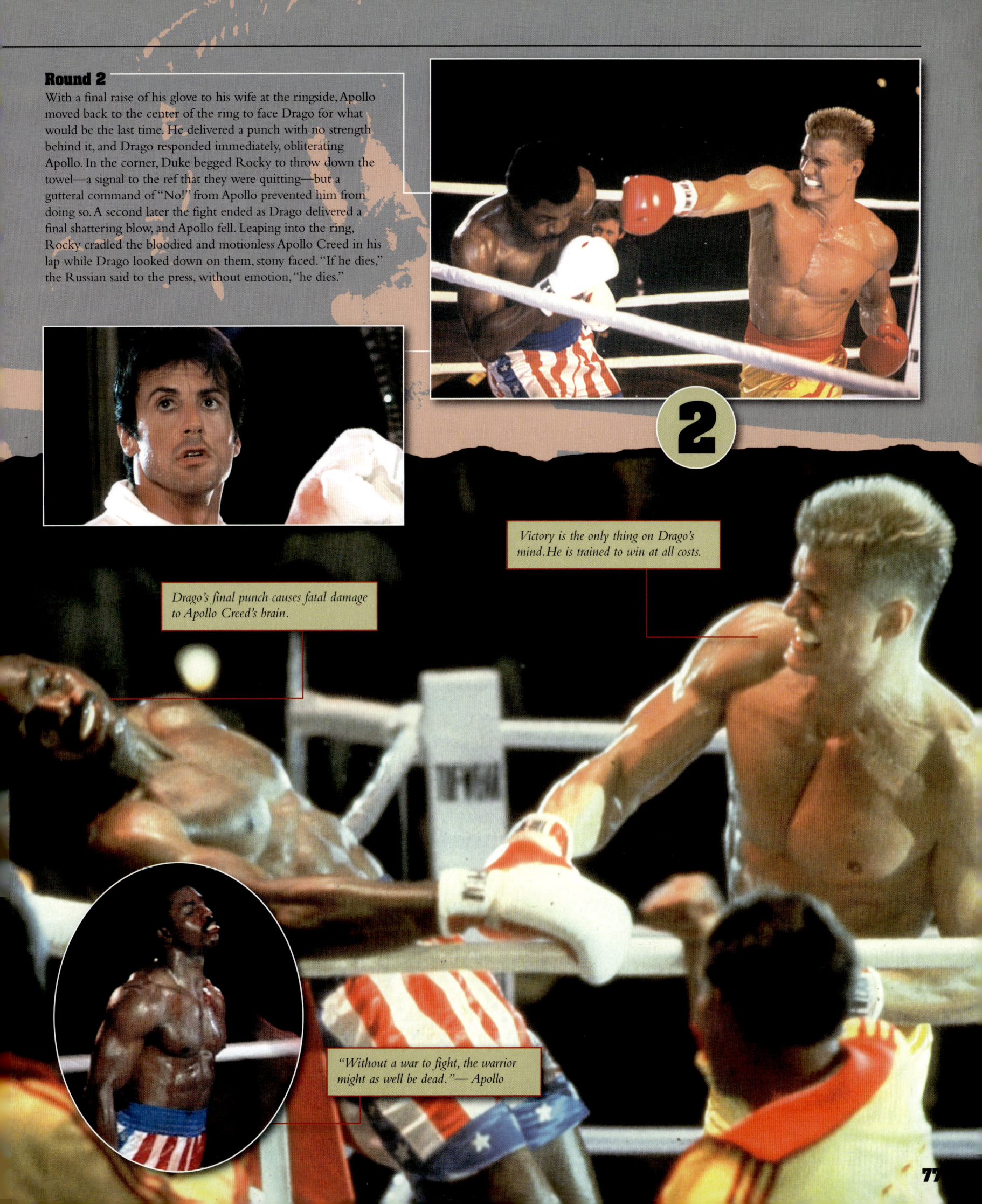

Round 2

With a final raise of his glove to his wife at the ringside, Apollo moved back to the center of the ring to face Drago for what would be the last time. He delivered a punch with no strength behind it, and Drago responded immediately, obliterating Apollo. In the corner, Duke begged Rocky to throw down the towel—a signal to the ref that they were quitting—but a gutteral command of "No!" from Apollo prevented him from doing so. A second later the fight ended as Drago delivered a final shattering blow, and Apollo fell. Leaping into the ring, Rocky cradled the bloodied and motionless Apollo Creed in his lap while Drago looked down on them, stony faced. "If he dies," the Russian said to the press, without emotion, "he dies."

Drago's final punch causes fatal damage to Apollo Creed's brain.

Victory is the only thing on Drago's mind. He is trained to win at all costs.

"Without a war to fight, the warrior might as well be dead."— Apollo

Tragic End

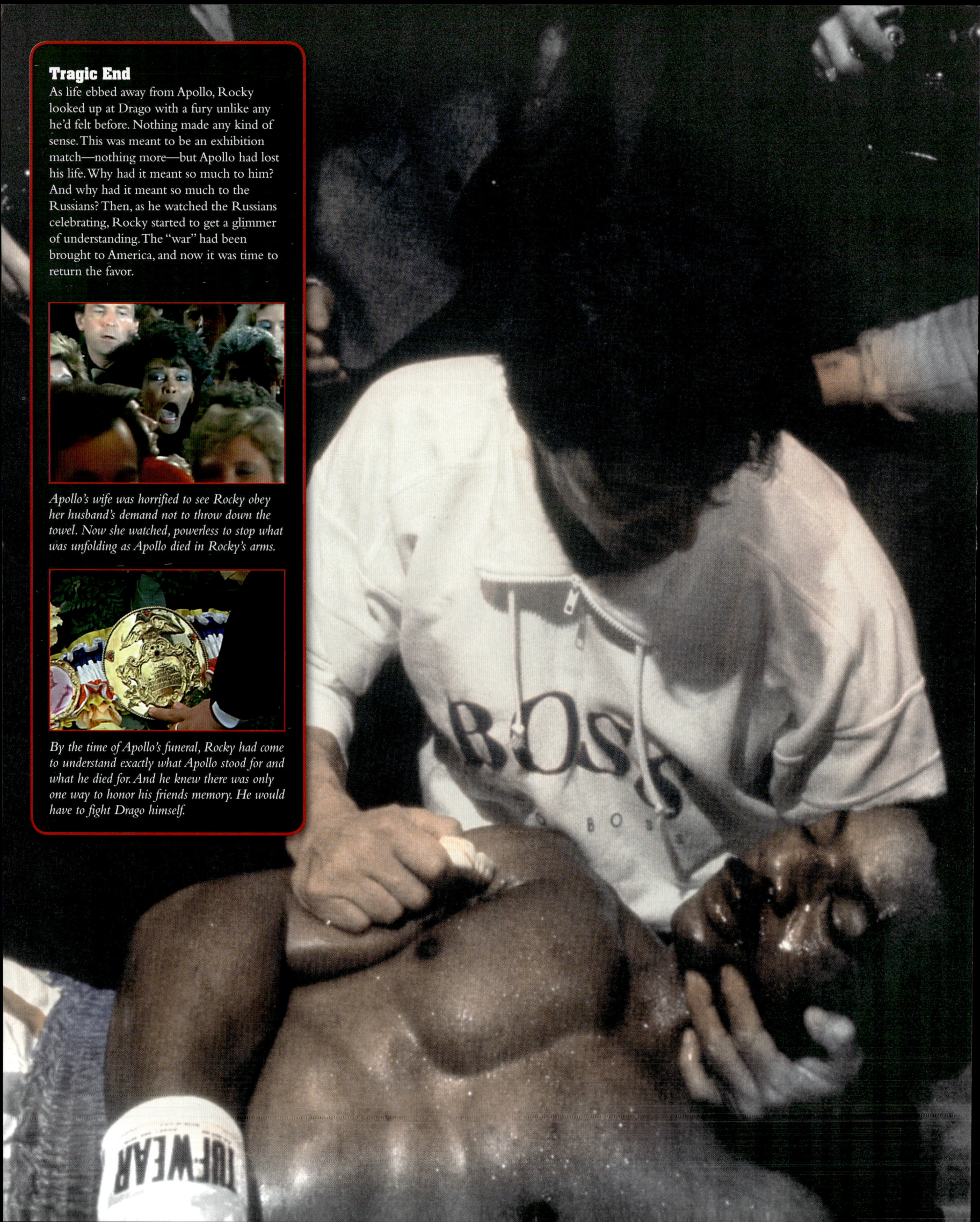

As life ebbed away from Apollo, Rocky looked up at Drago with a fury unlike any he'd felt before. Nothing made any kind of sense. This was meant to be an exhibition match—nothing more—but Apollo had lost his life. Why had it meant so much to him? And why had it meant so much to the Russians? Then, as he watched the Russians celebrating, Rocky started to get a glimmer of understanding. The "war" had been brought to America, and now it was time to return the favor.

Apollo's wife was horrified to see Rocky obey her husband's demand not to throw down the towel. Now she watched, powerless to stop what was unfolding as Apollo died in Rocky's arms.

By the time of Apollo's funeral, Rocky had come to understand exactly what Apollo stood for and what he died for. And he knew there was only one way to honor his friends memory. He would have to fight Drago himself.

West vs. East

"YOU KNOW HOW STRONG HE IS. YOU CAN'T WIN!" ADRIAN

EVERYTHING MOVED SO QUICKLY following Apollo's death. The Russians voiced sympathy for the 'unfortunate' events in the ring, but it was obvious that they were satisfied with the demonstration of Drago's prowess. Clearly, they would welcome a chance to defeat Rocky and prove Russia's ultimate triumph in the ring, and Rocky was more than ready to give them the battle they wanted. Initially he attempted to go by the book, but the boxing commission, fearful that the bout could result in another death, rejected his proposal. So, in a sensational move, he announced that he would give up his title and take the battle to the Russians on their own soil. The news came as a bolt from the blue to Adrian, who only learned what was happening from the reporters she found camped outside her home. Later, when Rocky returned, she confronted him, pleading with him not to go through with this. Having seen Drago in action against Apollo, she feared for her husband's life. Rocky responded that if Drago tried to kill him in the ring, he would have to be prepared to die himself.

The Announcement

At the announcement of Rocky's fight with Drago, Koloff seemed to confirm that the fight had become as much between two ideologies as two boxers when he stated that Rocky's defeat would be a symbol of how pathetic and weak Western society had become. As well as confirming that the fight would take place in Russia, Rocky revealed two more important elements: it would be held on Christmas Day, and Rocky wouldn't be receiving any payment, win or lose. He felt that this fight was about much more than just money.

Adrian Stays

Rocky did his best to explain to Adrian why he had to go through with the Drago fight, but although she could understand his reasons she couldn't accept them. Even if Rocky won, she argued, it wouldn't bring Apollo back. The couple had never been apart for long since the day they married, but for Adrian this was one battle too far. Reluctantly, she told Rocky she would not be accompanying him to Russia.

She loved her husband, but Adrian couldn't bear the thought of watching him die.

Welcome to Russia

"YOU REQUESTED THIS DUMB LOCATION?" Paulie

TO PREPARE HIMSELF for the fight with Drago, Rocky knew he would have to get away from everything that represented his regular life. This was a new breed of opponent—one whose background and mindset were alien from anything Rocky had ever encountered before, and he had to somehow prepare himself mentally as well as physically for the contest. Instinctively he knew that the answer was to live in Russia and to train there. Isolation was the key. So when he emerged from the plane onto the vast, snowy expanse of the Russian countryside, the only people with him were Apollo's trainer, Duke, and Paulie, the friend who had been with him from the beginning. The location Rocky had chosen was harsh and freezing, with the most basic living quarters and it is to Paulie's credit that he didn't step right back onto that plane and head for home.

Stepping out of the plane, Rocky was struck first by the cold, and then by the starkness of the environment. It was harsh but ideal for his purposes.

DUKE'S FAITH

Acknowledging that Rocky would have to do most of his training on his own, Duke assured the boxer that he had faith in him. He admitted that Apollo had been like a son to him and he knew that Rocky would honor his memory.

Rocky had specifically requested an isolated environment as his base in Russia. His feeling was that it would help him to focus his mind as well as toughen his body.

NATURE VS. SCIENCE

Neither Rocky nor Drago were taking the fight lightly and both of them were training as though their lives depended on it. But although their goals were the same, their training methods were radically different. While the Italian Stallion embraced nature and attempted to draw strength from it, Drago utilized the highest-end equipment that money could buy. Surrounded by his team, the Russian trained in a gym that in many ways resembled a science laboratory, filled with a myriad of machines and monitors. In stark contrast, Rocky trained alone, pitting himself against the harsh Russian environment and taking advantage of any natural obstacles he came across.

Drugs and Drago

While in America, the Russians had been adamant that Ivan Drago was a naturally trained boxer; that he was not artificially enhanced. They were lying. The truth was that all sorts of advanced steroids were being pumped into Dragos giving him almost superhuman strength. And these drugs, combined with the non-stop training, were having an effect not only on his body but on his mind. They were turning him into more of a machine than a man, stripping him of many of his basic emotions, and leaving him with nothing but life in the ring.

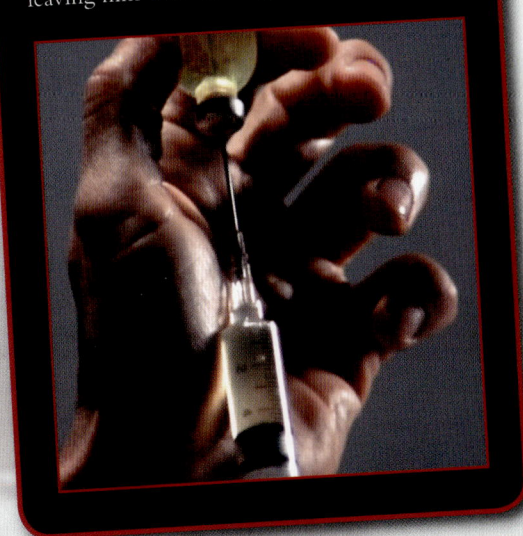

Out in the freezing cold, Rocky worked on building upper body strength by hoisting a tree trunk on his back.

Drago remained in the temperature-controlled gym, lifting barbells that held a series of tremendous weights.

Rocky found a new meaning for the term 'weight lifting' when he helped to pull a fallen cart out of the snow.

Drago's weights program was designed to target specific muscles. Machines monitored his progress all the way.

To boost his leg muscles, Rocky deliberately chose to run through the most difficult terrain he could find.

Surrounded by his keepers, trainers, and Ludmilla, Drago developed his running speed on the treadmill.

Chopping down trees helped Rocky build arm strength. Punching frozen beef was nothing compared to this.

Drago mowed down one sparring partner after another, each selected to challenge his abilities in different ways.

Hauling Paulie on a sled through deep snow was one of the most grueling exercises Rocky devised for himself.

Drago's training goals were similar to Rocky's, but he used hi-tech equipment to get optimum results.

81

Chaperones

Landing in Russia brought an unsettling feeling to Rocky, Paulie, and Duke. That feeling wasn't alleviated when Rocky was introduced to two burly looking men who were described as his chaperones. "Where you go," his Russian host said in a voice that reminded Paulie of Dracula's cousin, "they go." Rocky understood his meaning perfectly: whatever you do, we'll be watching. He would deal with it—in his own way.

For a time, Rocky played along, doing everything he was told to do. But he was just waiting for his moment…

That moment came during a mid-day jog, when Rocky suddenly took off, leaving the car stuck on the snowy road.

Fighting Fit

"I'M HERE WITH YOU, NO MATTER WHAT" Adrian

NONE OF THE PREPARATIONS Rocky had undertaken for his earlier fights could compare to this. Rocky remembered back to when he was training for his first fight with Apollo, and how he had deemed himself as ready as he could be when he was able to scale the steps leading up to the Philadelphia Art Museum. It had been at that moment when he had finally reached the top, that he had known in his heart that he was ready. For Drago, he needed to go further than he had ever gone before to prove himself. After losing his chaperones, Rocky headed off across country and began scaling the side of a mountain, as rapidly as he could. Driven by pure determination, he continued up and up, ignoring his bursting lungs and heavy legs, never looking back. Ultimately standing victorious on the mountain top, oblivious to the freezing temperatures, Rocky reached up to the sky and screamed out the name of his opponent: DRAGO!

A FAMILIAR FACE

From the moment he met Adrian, Rocky had an instinctive need for her approval. With it, he felt he could do anything, but without it he was distracted and somehow incomplete. Going to Russia without her was one of the most painful things he had ever done, so when, unexpectedly, she showed up, it was as if the final piece in a puzzle slipped into place. But why had she come? Adrian had been so emphatic that this time she couldn't support Rocky in his decision to fight. When Rocky asked her why she had changed her mind, she replied simply "I missed you."

> "YOU KNOW WHAT YOU HAVE TO DO. DO IT." Duke

No Pain

Paulie had been with Rocky from the beginning, and Duke had gotten to know him when he and Apollo served as trainers for the Clubber Lang rematch, but neither man had ever seen Rocky endure such grueling punishment in the name of preparation for a fight.

Heaven's Help
Kneeling down and saying a prayer before a bout was something Rocky had done for his entire life as a boxer. But now, for the first time, he found himself calling on the spiritual help of others: Mickey and Apollo. They had been the two people he was closest to in the boxing world. Now, he needed to feel as though they were in the ring with him, encouraging him on in what was undoubtedly going to be the toughest fight of his career.

Ready?

"IF I COULD BE SOMEBODY ELSE, I'D BE YOU" Paulie

AS ROCKY APPROACHED the arena, he understood for the first time how Drago must have felt in Las Vegas, walking into an environment that was completely alien and facing a crowd that really didn't like him. He forced himself to put that thought out of his head. It was a distraction, and he couldn't afford distractions at the moment. He needed to focus on taking Drago down, on honoring the memory of Apollo, and—despite his belief politics shouldn't enter the ring—on proving Russian propaganda wrong.

PAULIE'S HERO
Right before the fight, the normally unsentimental Paulie thanked Rocky for keeping him around when others would have dropped him and for giving him respect. "You're all heart, Rock" he added, genuine emotion in his voice, before advising Rocky to "Blast this guy's teeth out!"

Entering the Arena
Rocky's entrance was greeted by jeers from the audience. These people actually seemed to hate him, yet he had done nothing wrong. Their champion had come to his country and, in what was little more than a demonstration of might, murdered one of his best friends and a genuine American hero. It didn't seem right.

Avenging Apollo

"PUNCH 'TIL YOU CAN'T PUNCH NO MORE!" Paulie

As he entered the ring, Rocky was startled by the power of his own motivation—revenge, pure and simple. He needed retribution for Apollo's death and, in a way, he also felt that he was fighting for the American ideal. As for Drago, he knew that his handlers would regard defeat as a humiliation to their country, and was no doubt aware of his fate should he allow Rocky to win. But none of that mattered to him right now. He wanted victory. Not for Russia, but for himself.

Round 1
With the bell, Drago immediately stormed into action, determined to seize a quick victory and prove the weakness of Rocky and therefore America. Blow after blow from Drago's extended reach knocked Rocky off balance, causing him to drop to his knees. He was still in this position when Drago delivered another punch that sent him all the way down. Barely avoiding the 10-count, Rocky struggled back to his feet. With only one round gone, he was in trouble already.

Round 2
Back in his his corner, a stunned Rocky told Duke and Paulie that he was seeing three Dragos out there. (Paulie immediately suggested that he hit the one in the middle, advice that Duke surprisingly agreed with). The bell rang and Rocky went out to meet Drago again, but the Russian's relentless assault continued. Rocky could do nothing but try to stay on his feet and absorb the blows. At one point, perhaps out of frustration that he hadn't yet knocked out the American, Drago hoisted Rocky up and slammed him to the canvas. At that, a look of rage flashed across Rocky's face; a rage that allowed him to spring back to his feet. A frenzied exchange of blows culminated in a punch from Rocky that opened up a serious cut on the side of Drago's head. Everyone was stunned by the turn of events—not least the Russian himself.

Round 3-5
While Drago noted in his corner that Rocky could not be human, he must be made of iron, Duke was encouraging Rocky. "You hurt him. He's not a machine. He's a man!" But when the fight resumed Rocky was unable to follow up his brief resurgence and it seemed that Drago was taking back control, to the delight of the crowd and the Russian premier.

Round 6
It was beginning to look as though Rocky had weathered the Drago storm, at least for now. Seeming to find strength from hidden reserves, as he had done so often throughout his career, he delivered a large number of head and body blows that were obviously having an effect on Drago. For his part, Drago had not expected the fight to last this long, and his frustration showed. Perhaps it was at this point that the possiblity crossed his mind that Rocky might not just go the distance but he might actually win.

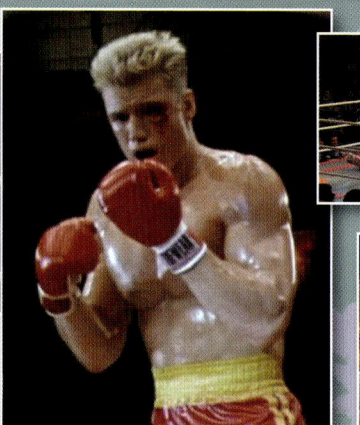

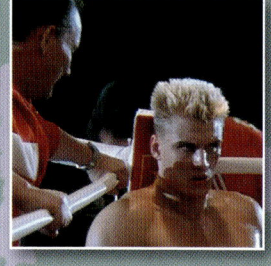

Round 7-9

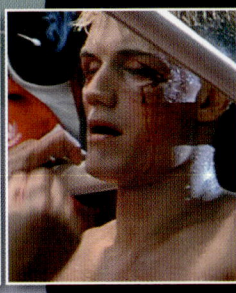

Throughout the seventh round, the fight seemed to go one way, then the other, and the toll it was taking on both men became increasingly obvious to everyone. In the eighth round, Rocky's blows were finding their targets more often, while in the ninth he was sent to the canvas by Drago, and he barely managed to groggily get back up.

Round 10

Both fighters were taking incredible punishment now. A series of blows delivered by Drago culminated in one that struck Rocky so hard in the face that a mixture of blood and spit was sent spewing from his mouth.

Round 11-13

As the two fighters continued to pummel each other with everything that they had, probably the biggest transformation in the latter part of the fight was on the part of the crowd itself. Amazingly, Rocky's raw determination seemed to be winning over the Soviets, as increasing chants of his name filled the arena.

Round 14

Both men seemed on equal footing, trading blows and each determined to knock the other out. But by the end, though, Drago definitely seemed to be gaining an edge.

"I FIGHT FOR ME...ME!!" Drago

Round 15

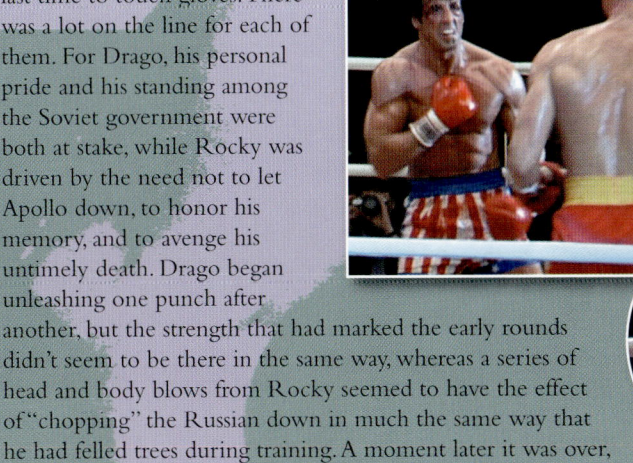

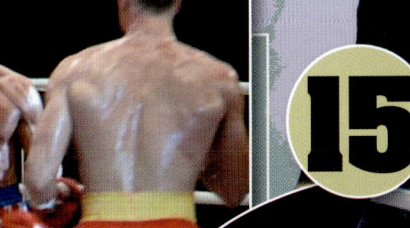

Rocky and Drago met for the last time to touch gloves. There was a lot on the line for each of them. For Drago, his personal pride and his standing among the Soviet government were both at stake, while Rocky was driven by the need not to let Apollo down, to honor his memory, and to avenge his untimely death. Drago began unleashing one punch after another, but the strength that had marked the early rounds didn't seem to be there in the same way, whereas a series of head and body blows from Rocky seemed to have the effect of "chopping" the Russian down in much the same way that he had felled trees during training. A moment later it was over, with Rocky proving victorious.

Rocky's final punch spins Drago on his feet before dropping him to the canvas.

Drago is counted out for the first time in his career.

Making Peace

"ROCKY BALBOA HAS DONE THE IMPOSSIBLE—AND THESE PEOPLE LOVE IT!" ANNOUNCER

AS DRAGO FELL, Rocky was aware of only two things: the pounding in his head and the Russian audience chanting his name. That was something he never would have predicted in a million years. He had come into this fight believing that the Russian people hated him as much as their officials seemed to. And maybe at first they had. Yet something in Rocky had connected with them, and here they were, cheering him on even though he had beaten their hero. Ignoring the strange feeling in his head, he made his way to the microphone in the ref's hand.

TALKING DETENTE

His words translated by the referee, Rocky began, hesitantly at first, to try to communicate to the crowd how he was feeling. What had begun as a need for retribution had gradually turned into a grudging respect for his opponent, the Russian people—even the Soviet Union itself. He explained how, throughout the fight, he could sense that the crowd's feelings for him were changing, as his were for them. It had been a kind of war, with politics coloring the world's views, but this night, he felt, could be a new beginning. "In here there were two guys killing each other," Rocky told the people, "But I guess that's better than 20 million!" His words were met by tumultuous applause.

Hearts and Minds

Despite the searing pain in his head, Rocky could tell that his words were having an impact on the crowd. But then something even more remarkable began to happen. Rocky saw Drago himself, along with Ludmilla, listening to him and nodding in appreciation. Most astonishing of all, the Russian Premier slowly got to his feet and began to applaud. One official after another followed his lead, then the crowd, until the whole arena was ringing with a standing ovation for Rocky. At that moment Rocky thought he had come up with the sequel to Apollo Creed vs. The Italian Stallion: The Italian Stallion Conquers the World.

Ludmilla had feared her husband's fate for having lost, but perhaps Rocky's speech would save him from punishment.

"IF I CAN CHANGE AND YOU CAN CHANGE, EVERYONE CAN CHANGE." Rocky

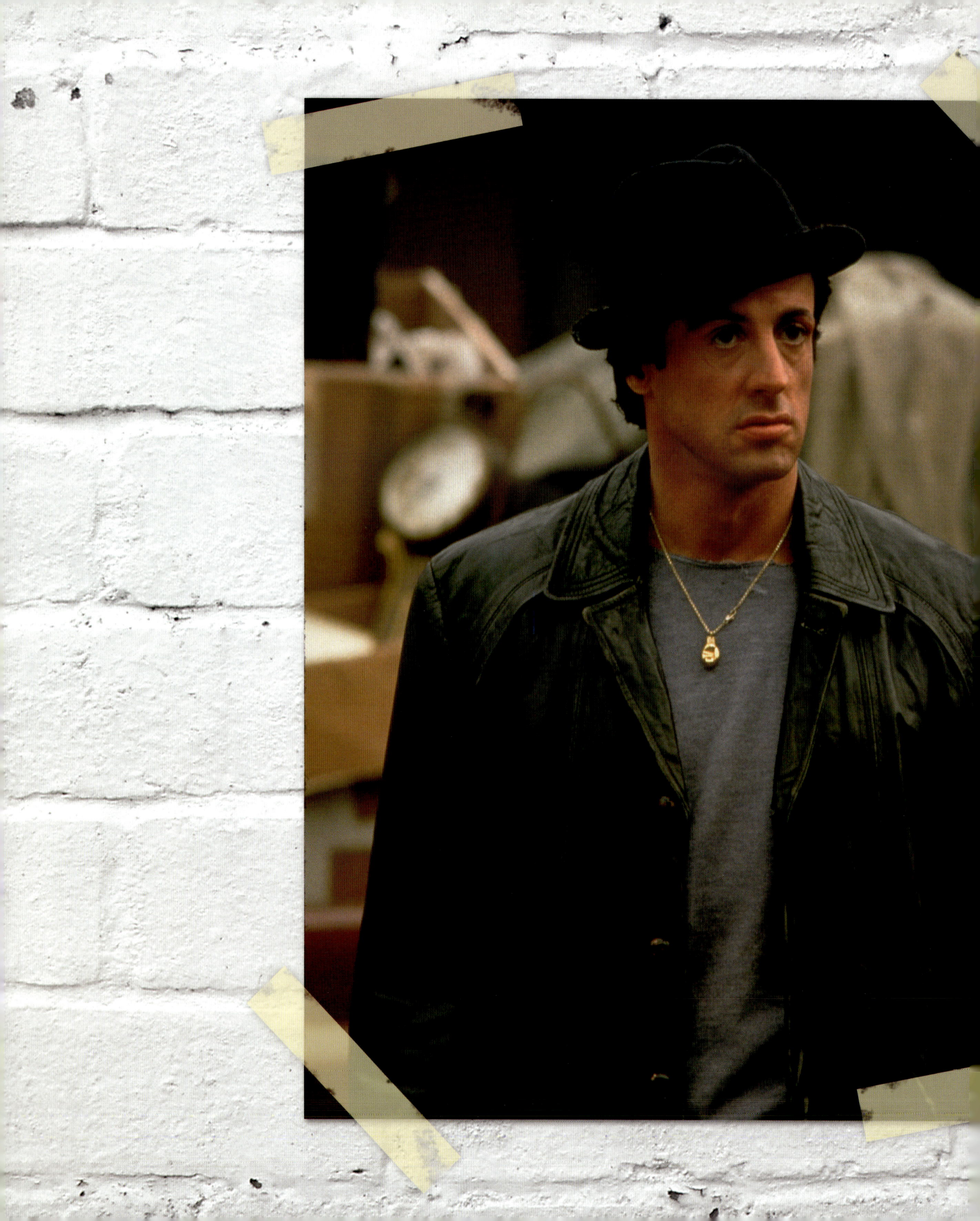

ROCKY V

SYLVESTER STALLONE SHOCKED the world, just as Rocky often did, when *Rocky IV* turned out to be the most successful movie of the whole franchise. It ranked near the top of the US and worldwide box office in 1985, making it one of the most successful sports movies of all time. But for all intents and purposes, despite the success, it seemed likely that Ivan Drago would represent Rocky's final match. However, five years later, yet another sequel was called for and it posed the awkward question—just what could it be about? Everyone involved decided that it was time to hit the 'reset' button, to essentially return Rocky to his roots by stripping him of the trappings of wealth, giving the character just enough brain damage to keep him out of the ring, and seeing how the family would survive as they were forced to go back to the beginning. To reinforce this notion, John G. Avildsen, who had directed the Oscar-winning original, was brought back to the helm of *Rocky V*.

Paying the Price

"ADRIAN, IT FEELS LIKE SOMETHIN'S BROKEN INSIDE!" Rocky

WHILE THE REST of the world was still savoring his victory over Drago, Rocky was nearly overcome with a wave of nausea. He put it down to the throbbing in his head he had felt at the end of the fight, but before long it was followed by other, more frightening sensations. He experienced moments when he'd forget, just for an instant, who Adrian, Paulie, and Duke were, and even where he was. Then just as quickly, reality would snap back into focus, and fear—an unfamiliar emotion—would take hold of him. Rocky didn't dare tell anyone about it, in case it made his fears real. When he stepped into the shower, he hoped that the cold water, would snap him out of whatever it was he was feeling and bring him back to his senses. It didn't work. Although he could hear Duke saying something to him—something about Apollo being proud—he was unable to make any sense of it. Out of the jumbled thoughts in his brain, only one thing would come into focus: Adrian. He desperately needed her. Adrian would make everything right. "Yo, Duke," he finally got the words out, "get Adrian!"

Confusion

While waiting for Adrian to arrive, Rocky stood in the shower, the icy water running down his face, and tried to pull himself together. He found himself thinking about Mickey and something he once said about changes happening to boxers sometimes. Everything seems okay, but then, right in the middle of a match, something goes wrong. It feels as though something inside the boxer's brain has broken and, according to Mick, the boxer is never the same again. The thought terrified him.

Duke was still celebrating the victory, unaware of what was happening to Rocky in the shower room.

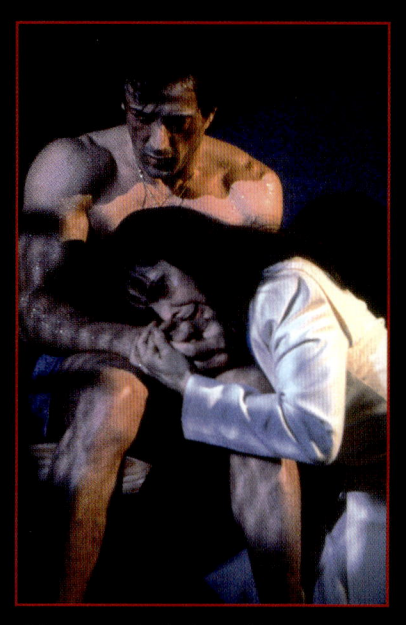

Adrian was shocked and frightened when she tried to comfort Rocky and he muttered, "Take me home, Mick."

BACK HOME

Getting on the plane in Russia Rocky still seemed fairly disoriented, but by the time he and his entourage arrived on home soil he was back to something of his old self. His speech pattern was a little off though, but Paulie optimistically put it down to the after effects of the Drago fight, and figured a good night's sleep at home would make everything alright. Adrian wasn't so sure; she had been with Rocky following every single fight he had since his taking the title from Apollo, and she had never before seen him behave the way he had back in the Russian shower room.

Conference Hijacked

Things took an unexpected turn at the post-fight press conference. Rocky had no sooner stepped up to the microphone than he was joined by flamboyant boxing promoter George Washington Duke and his protégé, an arrogant boxer named Union Cane. Armed with his own wireless microphone, Duke challenged Rocky to a fight against Cane. Before Rocky could say anything, Adrian jumped in, announcing that Rocky was retired and there would be no fight. Duke pushed the issue, and although Rocky wouldn't give an inch on the subject, it seemed the idea was a hit with the crowd.

George Washington Duke

"TIME TO PUT SOME HUSTLE BEHIND THIS MUSCLE." GEORGE WASHINGTON DUKE

IN HIS MIND, George Washington Duke epitomized the American dream, having started with nothing and built himself into a genuine boxing impresario. His success had been such that he had reached a point where he more or less owned the sport, never caring who he had to step on, use, or discard to get there. As he was fond of saying, "only in America" could you get ahead by crushing the competition. The one thing he had not been able to get control of so far was Rocky, but in watching his epic battle with Ivan Drago, Duke immediately saw an opening. With Apollo Creed gone as well as that old man Goldmill, Rocky would, he reasoned, no doubt be in need of guidance, and Duke felt he was just the man to offer it up—for a hefty cut of the profits any fight featuring Balboa would bring, of course.

RING MASTER

When it came to boxing—hell, when it came to anything, he often mused to himself—George Washington Duke was used to getting his own way. The fact that Rocky wouldn't give in to his needling and cajoling was something that ate away at him. It wasn't just because of the potential millions that he felt were within his grasp, it was more about ego. He couldn't remember the last time someone had rejected one of his overtures, and the fact that Rocky was doing so annoyed him beyond belief. But he wasn't the kind of man to take no for an answer. He'd get Balboa in the end—one way or another.

Temptations

There was pretty much no level to which Duke wouldn't stoop to get what he wanted. He had no problem with flashing expensive cars, promises of enormous paydays, and even beautiful women if it secured what he was after. And what never failed to amaze him was the willingness with which boxers dreaming of the big time would throw away their moral judgment in the pursuit of power and wealth.

George Washington Duke used a variety of expensive gifts to get boxers into his clutches.

Riches to Rags

"THIS IS NOT THE WAY IT'S SUPPOSED TO END;
IN HERE." ROCKY

Another Kind of Loss
As Rocky was saying goodnight to his son, he could hear a serious argument going on between Adrian and Paulie downstairs. Heading downstairs, he was met by the devastating news that Paulie had been tricked into giving power of attorney to the family's accountant while they were in Russia. The accountant in turn had disappeared with their millions. Rocky's mind was reeling. So much had happened recently— Apollo's death, the hastily organized trip to Russia, the victory over Drago. Who knew who was signing what?

Rocky blamed himself for giving Paulie the ability to transfer power of attorney in the first place.

The lawyer suggested a couple of prize fights would be enough to restore Rocky's fiscal status to what it had been.

Rocky wanted to take up the lawyer's advice, but Adrian, concerned about what happened in Russia, begged him to see a doctor first.

AS CRAZY AS IT SOUNDS, entering the doctor's office that day was more daunting to Rocky than walking into a boxing ring against even the toughest opponent. Maybe it was something to do with not wanting to hear his worst fears confirmed. He was only there because Adrian insisted, and although he instinctively knew she was right, a voice in his head was screaming for him to turn away and run as fast as he could. But as he looked at the pain in his wife's eyes, he realized he had to go through with this, no matter what the prognosis was. When the doctors came in with his test results, he could immediately sense the gravity of the situation from the way they were avoiding looking him in the eye. This was going to be bad. He took a deep breath and prepared himself for the worst.

Brain Damage
The doctors' words were devastating. Repeated blows to the head during Rocky's boxing career had resulted in irreversible brain damage. Probably, the bout with Drago had been one fight too many. Rocky's first instinct was to go into denial, claiming that he felt great, but even as he spoke the words he knew that they weren't true. It had been staring him in the face all along—the way everything had seemed different after the fight in Russia; his jumbled thoughts, the words that didn't come to him as easily as they had. He could no longer avoid the truth: his career was over.

The Auction

There was more bad news as the couple learned that the mortgage on their home was not paid off as they had believed. Added to that, it was discovered that Rocky owed six years of back taxes. There seemed to be only one solution: to sell the mansion and auction their possessions to pay off some of the debt. Everything seemed to be unravelling now in a way that left Rocky feeling completely helpless, and without boxing as an out, he had no idea where to turn or what to do. Instead, all he could do was watch as his life was taken apart piece by piece.

Rocky began to feel embarrassment about the excess of their lives. They had so much—almost too much—and they had let it all go.

Losing the motorcycles was one of the most painful things for Rocky. He wondered whether he and Robert would ever ride together again.

HOME TEAM

Rocky had always assured Adrian that their child would have everything that they missed out on growing up. His success in the ring had allowed them to give Robert everything he needed. Now, because of bad decision making, all of it was disappearing around them. He could see the pain on Robert's face and struggled to find the right words to reassure him that everything would be okay.

> "WE'VE BEEN THROUGH TOUGH TIMES BEFORE. DON'T WORRY, I'LL GET IT BACK!" Rocky

Mick's Place

"I'M GONNA BE LIKE AN ANGEL ON YOUR SHOULDER" Mick

THANKS TO MICKEY, the Balboas had at least one asset left. Shortly before his death, Mickey had drawn up a will in which he bequeathed his beloved old gym to Rocky's son Robert, so that alone was safe from the accountant's greedy fingers. Paulie too had something left—his house in the old neighborhood. In may ways it was like turning the clock back 20 years as Paulie and the Balboas returned to the place where it had all begun and prepared to start over. Shortly after moving back in, Rocky made his way over to the gym that had played such an important role in his success. As soon as he entered the old place, he was awash with memories and it was almost as though Mickey was right back there with him. Rocky fondly remembered the words of encouragement Mick had given him before his rematch with Apollo Creed, and cherished the memory of being given one of Mickey's most treasured possessions—Rocky Marciano's boxing glove cufflinks. His spirits lifted by thoughts of his old mentor, Rocky felt ready to go out and face the world once again. More than that, he had a plan.

"I DIDN'T HEAR NO BELL. NOW GET UP AND FIGHT THIS GUY HARD." Mickey

Turning Back the Clock

In Paulie's house, Rocky found a box that had been in storage for years. Inside were his old leather jacket, hat, and gloves. When Adrian joined him he was wearing them, and he had something else to show her: the glasses she had worn when they first met. Gently, he slipped them onto her face. In a moment, they were transformed into their earlier selves.

Memories of their first date and their first kiss came flooding back to Rocky and Adrian.

They realized that whatever happened, they still had each other. They had to keep things together for Robert's sake.

As the Balboas moved back in, the people from the neighborhood gathered round to welcome Rocky home.

ROCKY THE TRAINER

As he stood in Mickey's gym, Rocky began to feel that this place was his chance to give a little something back to the world. His career as a fighter might be over, but maybe there was a new role for him if he opened the doors of the gym to the public: as a source of inspiration to other aspiring boxers who dreamed of one day becoming a world champion. After all, it had happened before between Mick and himself—why shouldn't something similar happen again some day? Of course, he wasn't Mick, but maybe he could pass on something of Mick's teachings.

Tempted

Rocky knew that he had to stay out of the ring for his family's sake as well as his own, but he found himself continually being tempted, particularly by George Washington Duke. The promoter wouldn't leave Rocky alone, promising him a tremendous payday that would wipe out his debt and put him back where he had once been—on top.

Rocky was approached by a young man named Tommy Gunn, a boxer who wanted Rocky to be his manager.

They were interrupted by Duke, who mesmerized Rocky with his sales pitch until Adrian snapped him out of it.

"You're a damn fool," George Washington Duke sneered when Rocky rejected his offer.

ROCKY'S PUPPET

Rocky took a lot convincing before he agreed to become Tommy Gunn's manager. One of the reasons he finally decided to go for it were the similarities he saw between Tommy and himself in his younger days. Tommy was a good pupil, soaking up everything Rocky offered like a sponge and transforming himself as a fighter. The close relationship between trainer and student had a downside, however, with the media dismissing Tommy as being nothing but Rocky's puppet or clone. It ate away at the young fighter's deep-rooted need to establish his own identity, creating a rift that would later be gleefully exploited by Duke.

Tommy Gunn

"I JUST WANT TO SHOW YOU WHAT I'VE GOT" Tommy Gunn

ESCAPING FROM a background of family violence, Tommy Gunn traveled from his home in Oklahoma to Philadelphia with one aim: to convince Rocky to take him on as a student. When approaching his hero in the street got no results, the youngster decided to put his muscle where his mouth was and turned up at Mickey's gym. His talent and hunger impressed Rocky, who eventually allowed himself to be persuaded. Once committed, he embraced the task wholeheartedly, welcoming Tommy to his home as if he were one of the family. Clearly, Rocky felt he could bring out the champion in this young man in the same way that Mickey had with him. What he was seemingly blind to (although Adrian and Paulie could see only too clearly) was that Tommy was fundamentally different from Rocky. He was concerned with one person—himself. As Adrian would later tell Rocky, the one thing he couldn't give Tommy was heart, and without that, he could never be a champion of the people. But for a long time Rocky refused to see the truth, believing that Tommy had what it would take to achieve greatness.

TWO SIDES

As a child, Tommy had been a frequent victim of brutal beatings from his father. As if that were not bad enough, he also had to watch his mother undergoing the same treatment. Maybe that's why but there were two sides to him. The side he tried to present to the world was the affable one, the side that made him seem the kind of guy you'd want to hang out with. But then there was the darker side, where anger bubbled constantly beneath the surface—an anger that would erupt whenever he felt things weren't going his way.

CHANGING OF THE GUARD

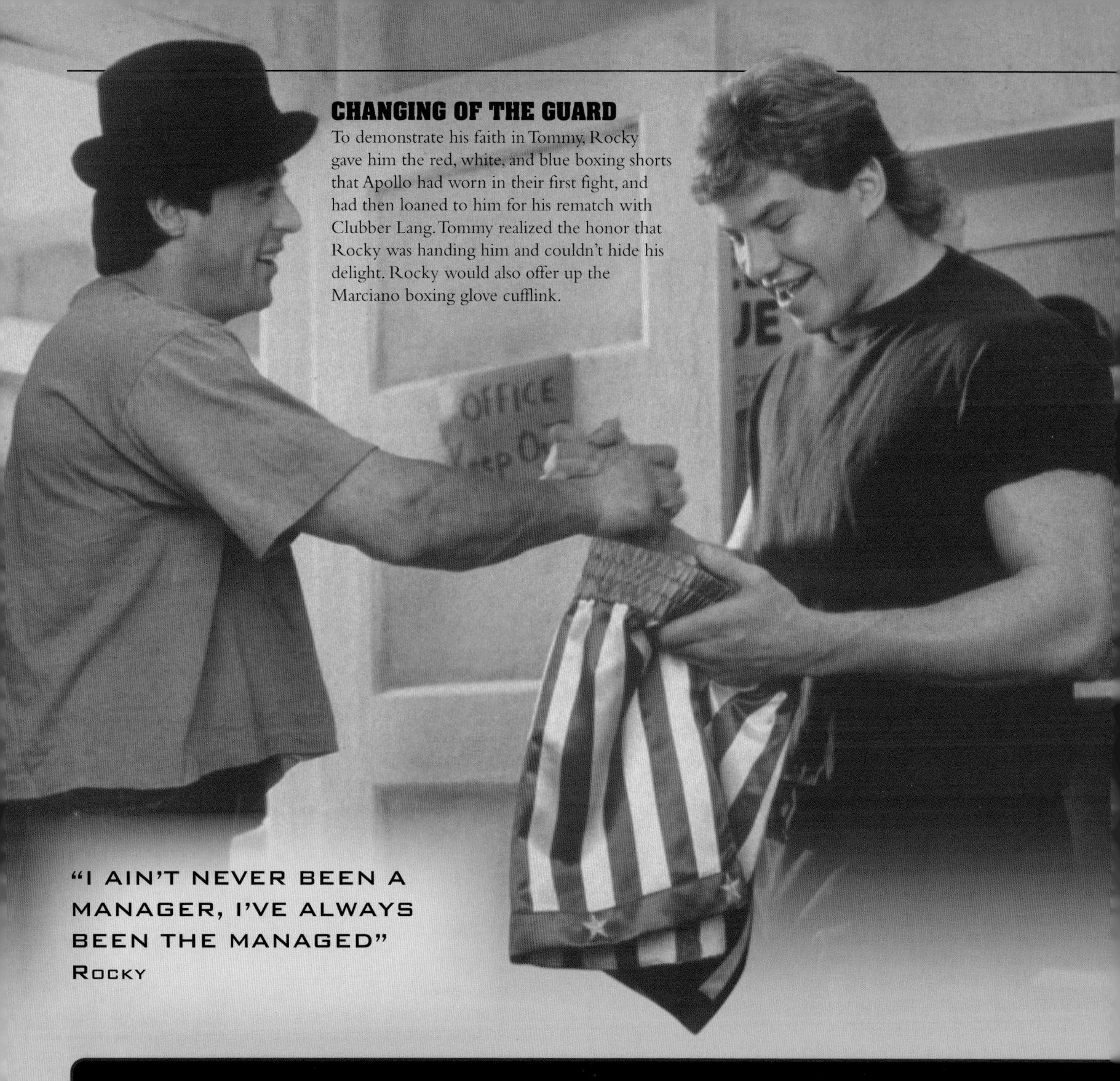

To demonstrate his faith in Tommy, Rocky gave him the red, white, and blue boxing shorts that Apollo had worn in their first fight, and had then loaned to him for his rematch with Clubber Lang. Tommy realized the honor that Rocky was handing him and couldn't hide his delight. Rocky would also offer up the Marciano boxing glove cufflink.

> "I AIN'T NEVER BEEN A MANAGER, I'VE ALWAYS BEEN THE MANAGED"
> ROCKY

The Next Step

Despite the progress he had made with Rocky, Tommy was becoming frustrated that he hadn't made much money yet and that he hadn't been given the opportunity to fight for the heavyweight title. Added to that was his irritation over the media's portrayal of him as being little more than Rocky's puppet. The solution to both problems seemed to come in the form of George Washington Duke, who was now pursuing Tommy as he had once pursued Rocky. If Tommy left Rocky and signed with him, he promised, he could make his dreams reality.

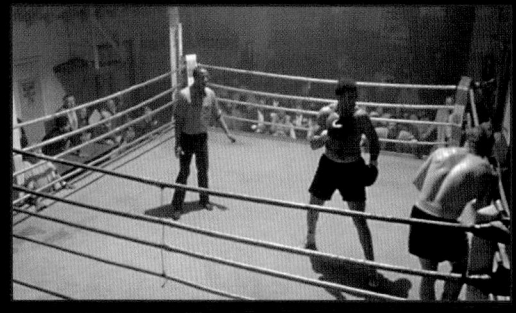

Under Rocky's tutelage, Tommy began to achieve more than he did on his own.

One victory followed another as Tommy gradually began working his way up the ranks.

Training Tommy

"THIS IS CALLED BOXING, IT AIN'T NO MUGGING" Rocky'

ONE OF THE REASONS THAT Rocky had, at first, been reluctant to manage Tommy was fear that he would do more harm than good to the younger fighter. Once he decided to train him, he realized the best way of going about it was to instill in the boxer all he had learned over the years. With this in mind, he began putting Tommy through similar routines to those he had gone through himself. They kicked off with a stop at the home of Father Carmine—the same priest who had married Rocky and Adrian some 15 years earlier—to ask a blessing in the hopes that things would go well. From there, they began daily jogs through the old Philadelphia neighborhood where, because of his connection with Rocky, the local crowds instantly embraced Tommy as one of their own. Things even reached the point where the duo ascended the steps leading to the Philadelphia Museum together, Rocky a bit more breathlessly than Tommy.

FIERCE AMBITION

Impressed with Tommy's development as a boxer, Rocky was nevertheless concerned about his impatience for the spotlight. He tried to chalk it up to youth, but he soon recognized, as Adrian and Paulie already had, that it was more than that. There was an arrogance to the boy, a reckless desire to go for the heavyweight championship before he was physically and emotionally ready. Rocky could see only too clearly that Tommy needed more experience, but it was someting the younger man just didn't want to hear.

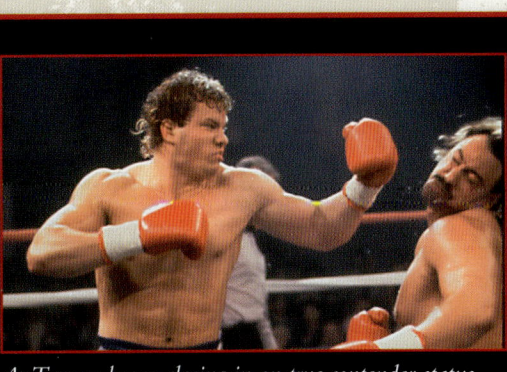

As Tommy began closing in on true contender status, Duke thought the time was right to make his move.

Duke arranged the perfect photo op, giving the impression that Tommy was already aligned with him.

When Tommy announced he was signing with Duke, Rocky desperately tried to make him see his mistake.

103

Family Life

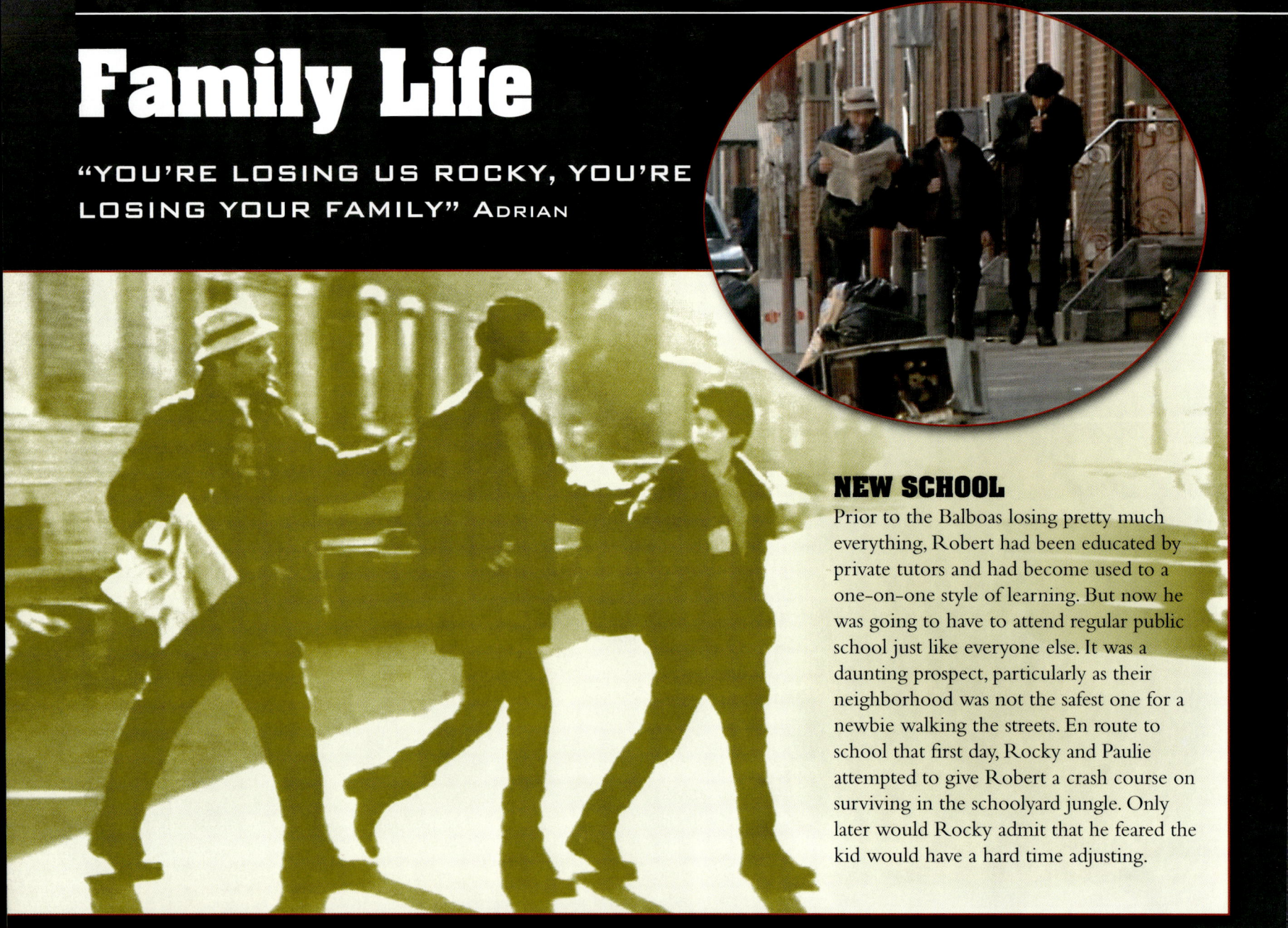

"YOU'RE LOSING US ROCKY, YOU'RE LOSING YOUR FAMILY" Adrian

NEW SCHOOL

Prior to the Balboas losing pretty much everything, Robert had been educated by private tutors and had become used to a one-on-one style of learning. But now he was going to have to attend regular public school just like everyone else. It was a daunting prospect, particularly as their neighborhood was not the safest one for a newbie walking the streets. En route to school that first day, Rocky and Paulie attempted to give Robert a crash course on surviving in the schoolyard jungle. Only later would Rocky admit that he feared the kid would have a hard time adjusting.

DESPITE ROCKY'S SUCCESS, his family had always been the most important thing in his life. The bond between Rocky and his son was particularly strong, the two of them referring to each other as the "home team." When the Balboas' fortunes changed, it was natural for the whole family to draw even closer together, rising to the challenge and doing what they could to make a bad situation better. The arrival of Tommy Gunn, however, changed things almost instantly. Overnight, Rocky seemed to distance himself from Adrian, Paulie, and Robert. Instead, he spent most of his time with Tommy, sharing boxing stories or imparting tricks of the trade. The change didn't go unnoticed, but any attempt to talk to him about it was met with denial. Rocky was so caught up in his new role that he couldn't see the damage.

From the first night that Tommy joined the Balboas for dinner, Adrian sensed a change in the family dynamics. It made her feel uncomfortable.

The Lost Boy

Things between Rocky and Robert seemed to be going from bad to worse. Not only did Rocky more of less kick Robert out of his basement "bedroom" so Tommy would have a place to stay, but he appeared to be oblivious to his son's struggles in school. It was as though he simply didn't care any more.

Robert had made his room a shrine to his father's triumphs, but Rocky was only interested in getting Tommy settled in.

Things weren't going well for Robert at school. He was targeted by bullies, who beat him up and stole his jacket.

Having had enough, Robert decided to fight back. Helped by Uncle Paulie, he started training at Mickey's gym.

Robert's delight at his victory against the bully turned to disappointment when Rocky showed little interest.

Rocky had no idea Robert was feeling so alienated, and was shocked when the boy confronted him about it.

Adrian finally got it through to Rocky that his obsession with training Tommy was causing him to lose his family.

Realizing his mistake, Rocky went to look for Robert and attempt to mend fences with him.

Heavyweight Champ

"HE'LL NEVER BE A ROCKY BALBOA!" Reporter

THE DREAM OF BECOMING a champion prizefighter was something that had driven Tommy ever since he was a kid. He followed the exploits of fighters like Apollo Creed and Rocky Balboa, and spent more time than he cared to admit imagining himself in the center of the ring, holding that championship belt over his head to the acclaim of the cheering crowd. And now his moment had come at last for Tommy, but the reality of that moment did not live up to his daydreams. While he had beaten Union Cane convincingly, the adulation of his dreams was replaced by the jeering of the crowd and the chanting of Rocky's name. Tommy was filled with a desire to get Balboa into the ring to prove to the world that he was a has-been.

UNION CANE

When Rocky had gotten off the plane from Russia, the press was awaiting his arrival, as was George Washington Duke and the number one contender, Union Cane. With the subtlety of a sledgehammer, Cane told Rocky he wanted to "take what you got" but the notion of a match was dismissed by the announcement that Rocky was retiring. In effect, the title was being handed to Cane on a technicality rather than a win. As a result, when Tommy agreed to work with Duke, he was first in line to take the title away from the new champ.

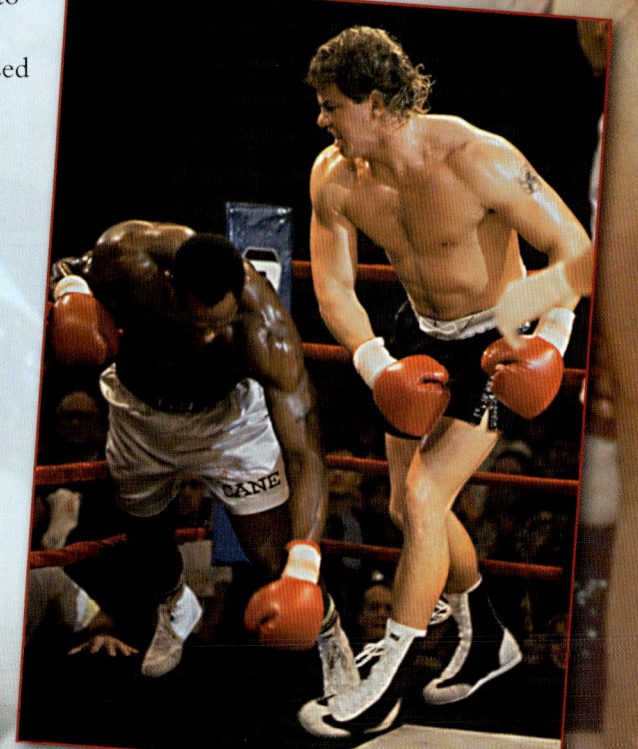

Initially Cane had given Tommy a tough time, but in the fight Tommy turned the tables on him.

Tommy's Big Fight

Rocky couldn't help but watch the fight and root for Tommy. Paulie, who was naturally rooting for Cane, jumped in his seat during the fight as Rocky started hitting the boxing bag, moving in unison with Tommy's movements on the screen before them. "He remembers everything," Rocky enthused.

Rocky was stunned when Tommy gave credit for his victory to Duke.

Duke's reaction to the jeering did nothing to calm the situation.

Meet the Press

In the post-fight press conference, Tommy was expecting praise from the media, but instead found himself on the defensive. Faced with hostile and dismissive questions, it seemed that no one was taking him seriously as the heavyweight champ. Tommy was angered by what he felt was an incredible lack of support.

Duke fielded questions from the press, seeming to know exactly which reporters to call on to inflame the situation.

If Tommy wanted respect, Duke reasoned, he'd have to get Rocky in the ring with him.

Later that night, Tommy arrived at the local bar, challenging a surprised Rocky to a fight.

Street Fight

"YOU'VE DONE PRETTY GOOD KNOCKING HIM DOWN. WHY DON'T YOU TRY KNOCKING ME DOWN NOW?" Rocky

WHEN TOMMY SHOWED UP at the bar and issued his challenge, Rocky nearly laughed in his face. He would have simply ignored him and walked away, until Tommy punched Paulie out. After ensuring that Paulie was okay, Rocky faced Tommy. Duke, for his part, had a thin smile, suggesting he knew exactly where this was heading. When Rocky proposed that Tommy try knocking him down, Duke interjected that Tommy Gunn only fought in the ring. "My ring's outside," Rocky snapped back, which led to the two men, followed by Duke, the camera crew he had brought along, and bar patrons heading outside.

Round 1

As the duo stepped into the alley, Tommy demanded respect, to which Rocky responded, "Come and get it!" With embarrassing speed, Tommy found himself pummeled by a series of blows that left him lying in a pile of garbage. Rocky, near tears, expressed his frustration and pain over the fact he and Tommy were supposed to be like brothers; and that he blew it all. Whirling around, Rocky nearly came face to face with Duke, who warned Rocky if he was touched, he'd sue. Walking away with Paulie and several others, Rocky was unaware that Tommy had gotten back to his feet and moved in with a series of vicious kidney blows that sent Rocky reeling. Stunned by the unexpectedness of the attack, Rocky left himself wide open for more.

Round 2

For the moment, Tommy was on fire, hitting Rocky with everything he had been taught. Rocky, whose brain felt like it was going to explode with each blow, suddenly felt as though he were back in the ring with Drago. As the assault continued, he barely noticed that the crowd was growing larger, and that Adrian and Robert were there as well—having actually seen Rocky fighting on TV! On the pavement, Rocky felt himself slipping into oblivion, until he suddenly had a vision of Mickey standing there, demanding that he get up and "fight this bum hard." For one last time, Mickey was as he described himself to be—an angel on his shoulder, encouraging him to get up when getting to his feet seemed like an impossibility.

"YO, TOMMY! I DIDN'T HEAR NO BELL... ONE MORE ROUND!" Rocky

"MOM... MOM! DAD'S ON TV AND HE'S FIGHTING!" Robert

Round 3

As Rocky stood demanding a final round, Tommy was willing to oblige, and threatened to smash him through the pavement this time. Tommy moved in for the attack, but Rocky leaving the rules of boxing behind him for the moment, turned their struggle into a genuine street brawl. Reinvigorated by this vision of Mickey urging him on, and furious with himself for jeopardizing his relationship with his family over someone the caliber of Tommy Gunn, Rocky was back on form, jabbing, punching, utterly decimating his opponent. Tommy was defenseless against Rocky's onslaught and as a result was knocked virtually unconscious. Rocky had proved to Tommy, to George Washington Duke, and to the world—thanks to the cameramen who had captured the moment—that he was still the undisputed heavyweight champion.

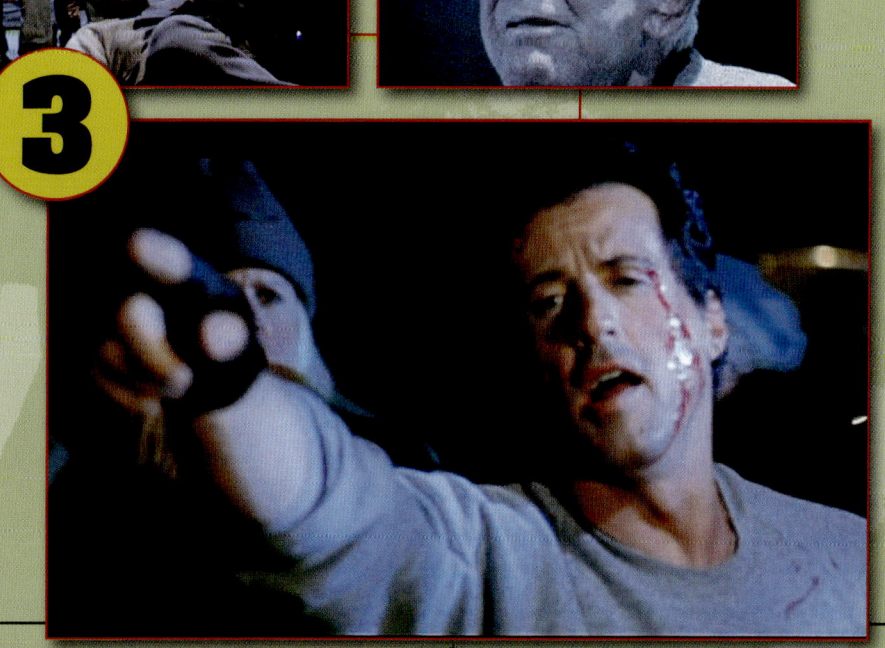

109

Rocky Wins

"WE WERE SUPPOSED TO BE LIKE BROTHERS, TOMMY! YOU BLEW IT!" Rocky

ADRIAN WATCHED the fight unfolding before her with a sense of dread as well as perhaps a tiny bit of joy. She feared what the results could do to Rocky, but couldn't fight the feeling that Tommy had all of this and more coming to him after the way he had participated in tearing her family apart. When it ended with Tommy seemingly slipping in and out of consciousness, she was filled with happiness as Rocky spoke to her and seemed perfectly fine. It was the opposite of what she had experienced with him in Russia following the fight with Drago.

Having gotten his second wind, Rocky called for "one more round" with Tommy.

Rocky came back fueled by the rage that had been building within him toward Tommy.

Despite a few desperate punches, Tommy was largely powerless against Rocky's assault.

The fight came to an end as Rocky slammed Tommy against the front of a bus and knocked him out.

As Rocky approached, Duke warned him off with the words, "Touch me and I'll sue!"

As Duke went sailing across a car hood, Rocky asked, "Sue me for what?"

REUNITED

Having proven himself against Tommy—demonstrating to everyone that he was the true champion—Rocky moved on to embrace what he finally recognized as the most important part of his life, his family. As they began the walk home, Rocky wasn't sure of the future, though he was fairly confident he would never box again. It seemed as though that part of his life really was over. But the question remained, what would Rocky Balboa do next?

Father and Son

One of the positives to come out of the whole Tommy situation was the strengthening of Rocky's bond with his son. He had learned to genuinely appreciate Robert for who he was. As they raced to the top of the stairs of the art museum, Rocky prayed that they would always be this close; that nothing would come between them again.

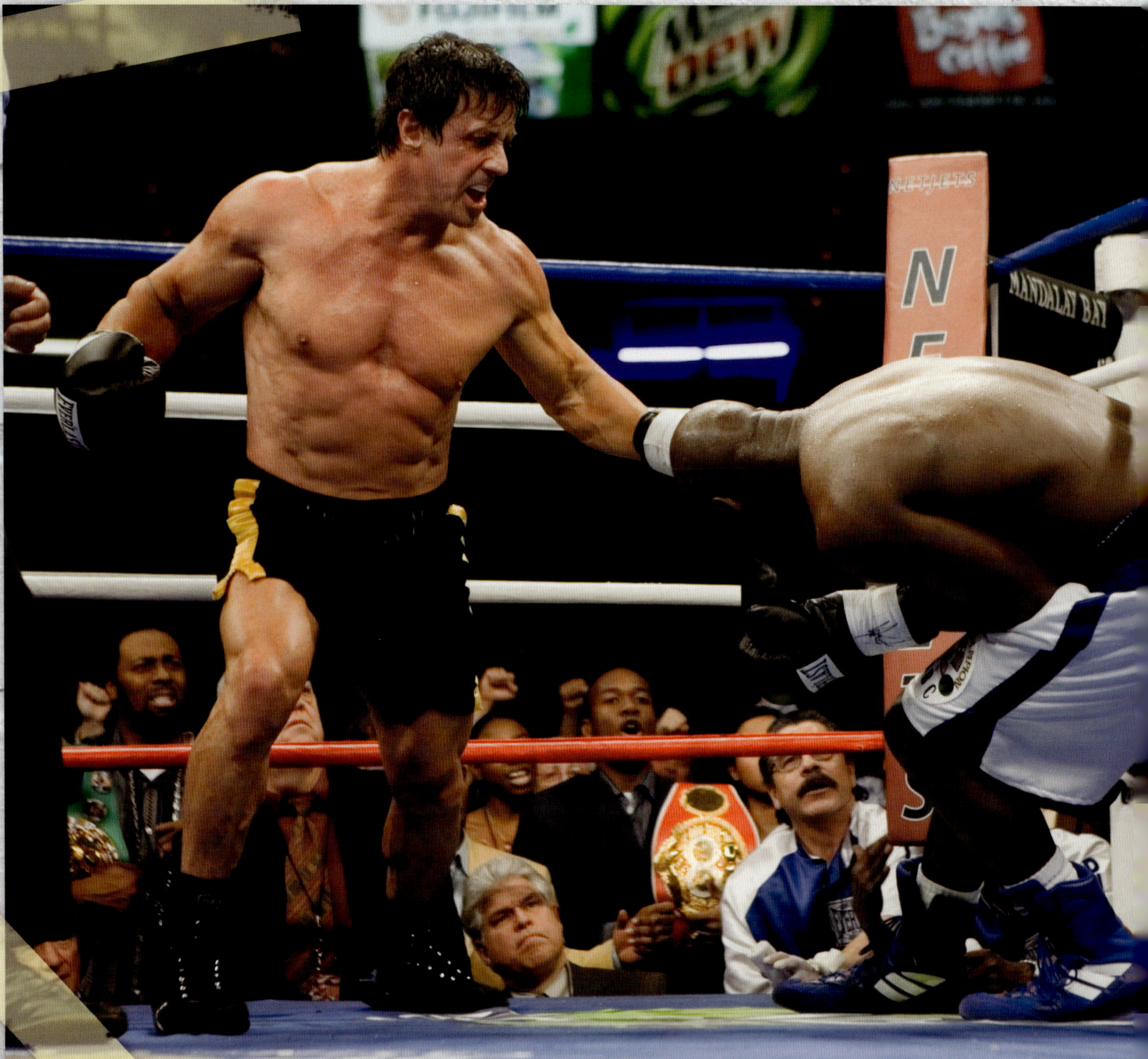
MANDALAY BAY

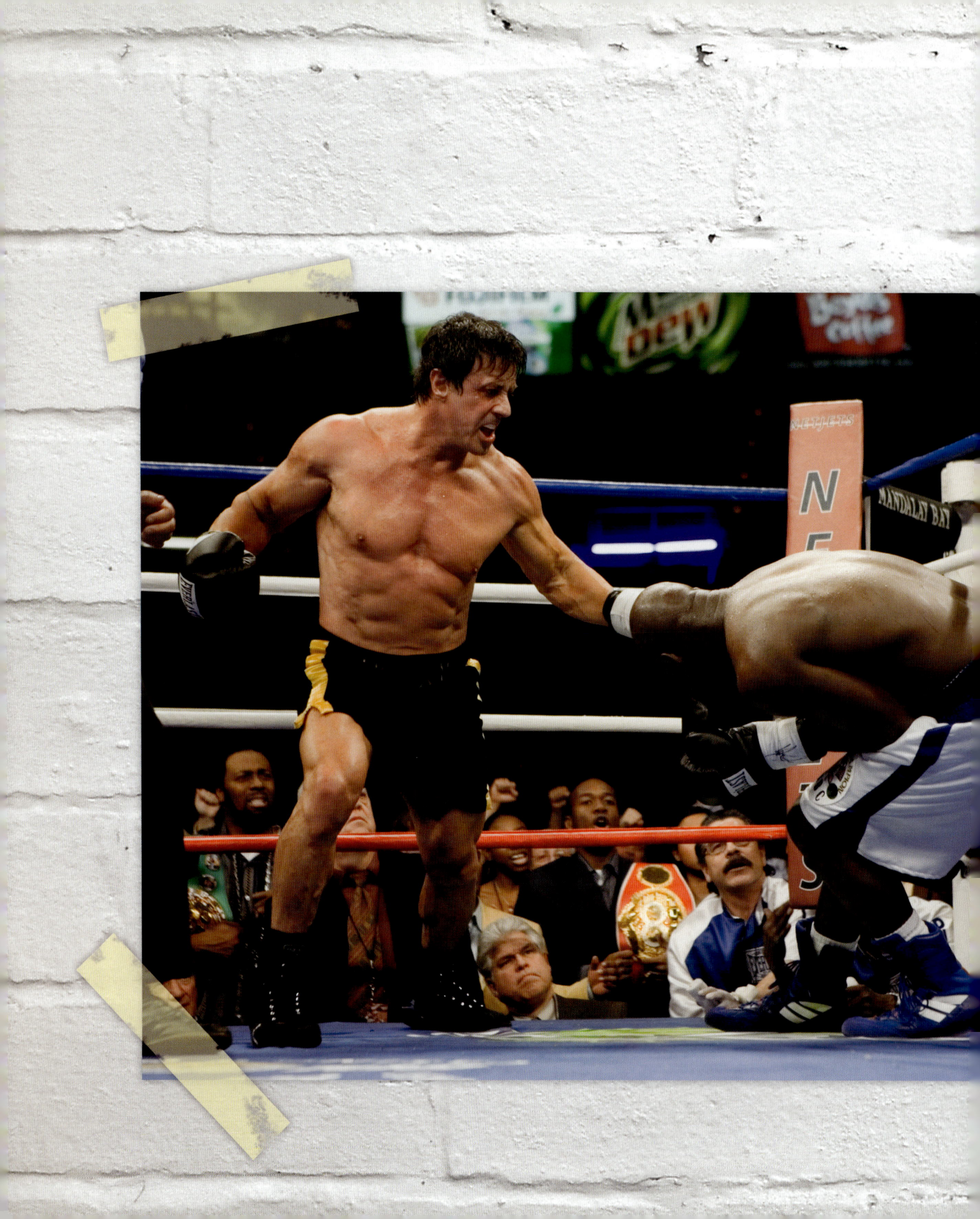

ROCKY BALBOA

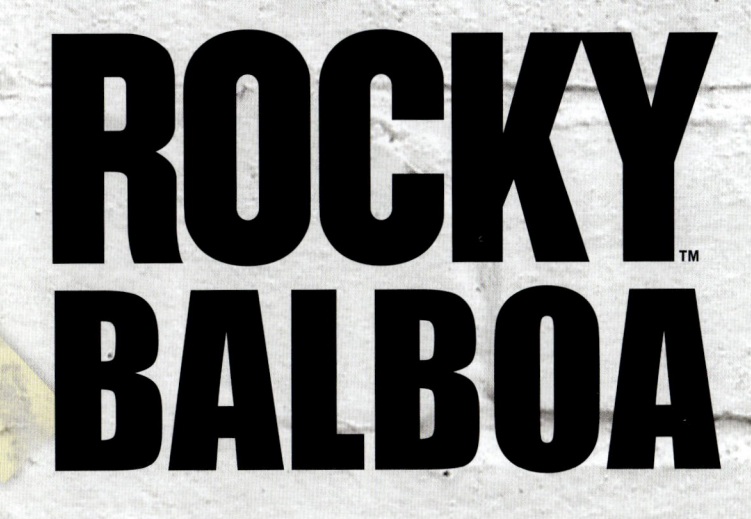

In many ways, the themes and events in the Rocky films seem to reflect Sylvester Stallone's own life, and that is true more than ever for *Rocky Balboa*. When the movie was announced, the news was greeted with a mixture of enthusiasm and skepticism. Some fans welcomed the idea, but others doubted whether Stallone could pull off another Rocky movie, 15 years after the last one. Similarly, in the movie itself the world wonders if Rocky can get back into the ring after such a long absence. The answer in both cases is a resounding yes. The idea of the underdog taking on the champion of the world, which struck such a memorable chord in *Rocky,* also underpins *Rocky Balboa*. An older and wiser Rocky feels that he still has something left to give in the ring and with the courage and determination that fans have come to know and love, he proves that he can still go the distance. For both Stallone and Rocky, the result is a triumphant return.

Rocky's World

"I DON'T WANT YOU TO THINK NOTHIN'S OFF. MY WIFE – SHE'S GONE, BUT SHE ISN'T." Rocky

Remembrance
Every year on Adrian's birthday, Rocky made a special pilgrimage to her grave, determined to mark her birthday in death just as they had celebrated it in life. It had been three years since she'd passed away from ovarian cancer, but her loss remained an open wound that wouldn't heal, no matter how hard he tried.

WITH TOMMY GUNN out of their lives, the Balboa family became stronger. Robert grew up and eventually started work in an office, while Paulie went back to the meat plant. For Rocky and Adrian, it was a time where they could truly focus on putting their lives together again, helped in part by the return of some (although not much) of the money that had been stolen from them by their accountant. Their true saving grace was their relationship and Rocky and Adrian's love intensified with age, rather than diminished. All that they had once had—the money, the mansion, the cars, the fame—didn't matter as long as they had each other. But when cancer struck, Rocky no longer had Adrian. Seemingly overnight she was gone, and a grief-stricken Rocky was left to face the world alone. He would cherish the memory of their 27 years together, while biding his time until he was reunited with Adrian.

New Purpose

He wasn't sure how or why it happened—maybe Cuff and Link provided the inspiration—but it suddenly occurred to Rocky that it might be a good idea to use Adrian's life assurance, plus some of his savings to open a local restaurant.

Rocky's

The concept of the Italian restaurant was simple. Memorabilia from Rocky's career, including a mural of himself and Apollo Creed in the ring, would be strategically positioned around the place so customers could enjoy a pleasant atmosphere, good food, and the occasional story from the former two-time Heavyweight Champion of the World. What most people didn't realize, was that this restaurant was also something of a lifeline for Rocky, a safety net to prevent him from drowning in loneliness.

Rocky's old adversary, Spider-Rico became a regular fixture at the restaurant.

Family and Friends

"YOU LIVE SOME PLACE LONG ENOUGH, YOU ARE THAT PLACE" Rocky

WHEN ROCKY WAS younger, he didn't need anyone else. He had been on his own for so long, that he thought it was the way things were supposed to be. But then Adrian came into his life and showed him that things could be different. Now, with Adrian gone, there was a void in Rocky's heart that he needed to fill. Not a romantic void, per se, but more of an innate need to be with others. Despite still having Robert and Paulie, Rocky knew it would be easy to become introverted, so he opened the restaurant and forced himself to face the world. What he found strange, however, was the way the past kept catching up with him even while he was trying to move forward. Spider-Rico, who he had barely seen for three decades, simply showed up at the restaurant one day and became a regular fixture. Perhaps motivated by the feeling that the man's somewhat destitute place in life could have so easily been his own, Rocky made sure that the former boxer had whatever he wanted to eat and drink.

Blast from the Past

The last time Rocky had seen "Lil Marie," he was a two-bit brawler with big ideas and she was a 13-year-old kid hanging out on a street corner with a bunch of neighborhood punks. He'd insisted that she allow him to walk her home and along the way he had tried to give her some important life lessons. But instead of gratitude she had responded with the stinging words: "Screw you, Creepo." But now Lil Marie was all grown up, as Rocky discovered when he caught sight of her waitressing at *Andy's Bar*. Although Rocky's dire predictions for Marie's future had not come true, she did not have much in her life, apart from her sixteen-year-old son Stevenson, more commonly known as "Steps." Gradually a close friendship developed between the single Mom and the lonely widower at a time when they both needed it most.

Rocky reappearance made a genuine difference to Marie's life. Along the way he even managed to strike a rapport with the troubled Steps.

Marie was grateful for Rocky's presence—her son needed a strong male role model.

Paulie

Paulie Pennino was one of life's constants. No matter how many years had passed, the man himself barely changed. Maybe he was a little stouter, a little grayer, and a little more lined but he was still the same old lovable grouch. But recently Rocky had noticed a change in Paulie. Although he was in a relationship with a woman, Paulie was also still wrestling with guilt about his sister Adrian. As he and Rocky visited areas of Philly important to Rocky and Adrian, just as they did every year on her birthday, Paulie finally admitted that these visits were painful to him. "You treated her good," Paul said to Rocky. "You had the good times. I treated her bad. I don't need to be thinkin' about this." More than anything, Paulie just wanted to get as far away from the past as he possibly could.

In many ways Rocky and Paulie were like brothers—although they loved each other, they fought frequently.

Punchy

Deciding he wanted a dog, Rocky, accompanied by Marie's son Steps, went to an animal shelter and found a scruffy-looking older mutt. Steps suggested he get something less ugly and younger, but Rocky didn't agree. "It's a nice ugly!" Rocky replied. "There's mileage left on this animal." Words that could just have easily been applied to himself as to Punchy the dog.

Robert

Although Tommy Gunn had come between Rocky and his son for a time, they eventually reconnected and ultimately grew closer than ever. But time passed, Rocky's career faded into history, and the legend of all he had accomplished began to build, and Robert found that he was distancing himself from his father once more. The reason? People always looked at him or treated him differently once they knew his last name and discovered that Rocky was his father. Even his office job was a result of who is father was rather than a testament to his own ability.

Robert struggled to create his own identity, separate from his father's achievements.

Rocky thought that the growing distance between them was because Robert was embarrassed by him.

Mason "The Line" Dixon

"PEOPLE LIKE YOU—THEY GOTTA PULL THEMSELVES WIDE OPEN AND SEE WHAT'S LIVIN' INSIDE." MARTIN, MASON'S FORMER TRAINER

THE PROBLEM WITH FAME and all of the trappings that come with it, is that once you have a taste of it, you can't help wanting more. Heavyweight Champ Mason "The Line" Dixon was gradually learning that fame and glory came at a price and in his case, it was his self respect that had been sacrificed. The veil truly began to be lifted from his eyes during his latest fight, which took place in Las Vegas. Like most of his bouts it was over almost as soon as it began—inferior opposition quickly disposed of in yet another easy title defense. But instead of the expected roar of approval from the crowd Mason was jeered and trash was thrown into the ring. Later, upon watching the playback of the fight on television, he heard one ringside commentator refer to the bout as "another disappointing title defense," with another adding, "It was just a matter of time." The response baffled him; what exactly did these people want from him? More importantly what did he want from himself. Such questions began to gnaw away at Mason Dixon.

Seeking Answers

Mason needed some answers and he turned to the one person he knew he could always count on—his former trainer, Martin, who had trained him since he was a kid. As Mason had become more successful new, more powerful advisers persuaded him that he didn't need his old trainer anymore. Martin, an elderly man, still running his dilapidated gym, understood the problem at once—Mason needed to restore his pride in himself.

Self Respect

Martin felt that changing the outside world's opinion of Mason wouldn't happen overnight, but changing the way he thought about himself, well it was never too late for that. Mason needed a challenger who wasn't afraid of him, one who would be a real match for him. "The only time people know what they're really made of is when they're getting hurt." Martin pointed out. Mason took Martin's words to heart, little realizing how prophetic they would turn out to be. Fate was about to offer Mason the chance to test himself against a true contender.

Man vs. Machine

"YOU THINK YOU OUGHTA STOP TRYING THINGS 'CAUSE YOU HAD TOO MANY BIRTHDAYS? I DON'T." Rocky

IN THE SERIES "MAN VS. MACHINE" ESPN picked a pair of athletes from two different eras and pitted them against each other in a virtual reality contest. Using the same rules, the same equipment, and making the contenders the same age, it tried to find out who would win a hypothetical contest. In its most recent episode, it brought Rocky Balboa in his prime together with current champ Mason "The Line" Dixon, and let their computer-generated alter egos slug it out. In the end, the computer decided that Rocky would triumph in the 13th round by knocking Mason out. What no one suspected as the show aired was that what started out as a bit of entertaining conjecture would have a real-world impact. To begin with, it inspired heated debate between boxing fans and sports commentators. Soon Mason and his team suddenly found themselves in the ridiculous position of having to argue the computer's decision. While Mason dismissed the technological fight as little more than a meaningless sci-fi gimmick, for his part, Rocky found himself watching the television mesmerized, completely swept up in what was unfolding.

The Challenge

Rocky came away from watching the fight filled with a desire to get back into the ring and to pull himself out of his current lonely and lethargic life. "Nothin' big," he told Robert. "Small things. You know, mostly local." The idea was met with ridicule from his son and pretty much everyone else who heard it, all of whom thought that Rocky was too old and indeed, must have taken too many blows to the head during his career. Mason's people, however, had ideas of their own.

Sports commentators were split in their feelings over the computer's determination as to who would win.

Watching the fight, Rocky experienced feelings that he thought had died a long time ago.

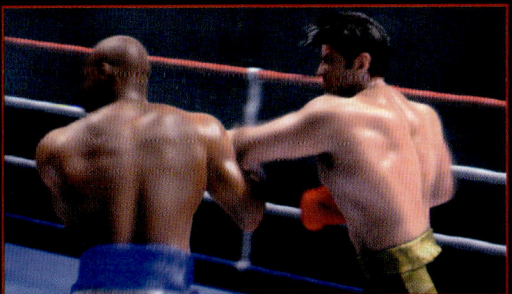

The CG fight went 13 rounds with Rocky and Mason hitting with everything they had.

In the end, the computer proclaimed Rocky the winner—a controversial decision.

Running with the "buzz," Mason's people proposed an exhibition bout between Mason and Rocky.

121

Meet The Press

"YOU REALLY DON'T KNOW MUCH ABOUT NO-BODY UNTIL YOU LEND 'EM MONEY OR PUNCH 'EM HARD." Rocky

ROCKY WAS AMAZED to be sitting at the press conference, with Paulie and Duke—who had agreed to train him—by his side, and Mason and his team on the other side of the podium. Fielding questions from the press (who had gotten more aggressive than he remembered), listening to Mason fight off cheap shots thrown his way, even the defenses he offered to justify getting back into the ring at his age, all of it was incredible. And it had not been an easy ride. Getting Duke on board was simple enough, but convincing the boxing commission to re-license him was more of a problem. However they did in the end, as their state-of-the-art medical equipment revealed that the brain damage detected back in 1990 was not as severe as originally believed. Mason, on the other hand, definitely projected a different frame of mind. Rocky suspected that he didn't really want to be involved in this media circus and Rocky didn't blame him. Putting himself in the champ's position, he wasn't really sure if he would feel so differently. While the aging ex-champ had little to lose and possibly much to gain from this fight, Mason was putting his whole career on the line.

Media Circus

The constant criticism finally got to Mason, who demanded to know what the press wanted from him. "No matter what I do," he claimed, "it's never gonna be enough, because you say so….You make people's reputations and then when you want to take 'em away, you do just that." He acknowledged he'd made mistakes along the way and would likely make more, but the one thing he couldn't reconcile with was their obvious wish that he was somebody else.

FIGHTING CHANCE

After agreeing to the bout, Rocky suffered a major crisis in confidence. He wondered if he had spent too much time shooting his mouth off without considering whether or not he could live up to his words and realize his full potential. In the end, inspiration came from a surprising quarter and it was Marie who turned things around for Rocky. In many ways she reminded him of Adrian in the way she was able to see things clearly and put him on the right track. She demanded that Rocky not move aside for anyone, that he, instead, make them move for him.

"You're a fighter, right?" she asked. "Fighter's fight."

Back In Training

"WHENEVER YOU LAND A SHOT, IT'S GOT TO FEEL LIKE HE TRIED KISSING THE EXPRESS TRAIN." Duke

ROCKY'S SELF BELIEF was fortified by the coming together of his "team." As always, Paulie was right by his side and once again Duke was willing to train him. But more importantly, Robert had managed to put aside his own insecurities, quit the job he was miserable in, and expressed a desire to be in his father's corner for the fight. However, despite having a great backup team, Rocky still faced the enormous task of getting ready for the fight. As Duke pointed out, although there was nothing about fighting itself that Rocky didn't already know, the speed necessary to defeat Mason simply wasn't an option, given Rocky's age. And this wasn't helped at all by the fact that he had arthritis in his neck and calcium deposits on most of his joints. As far as Duke was concerned, there really was only one option left—they would have to change the emphasis from the way that Rocky used to fight and focus, instead, on creating good, old-fashioned blunt force trauma. "Heavy duty cast iron pile drivin' punches that will have to hurt so much it'll rattle his ancestors," Duke emphasized. The goal was to start building some "hurting bombs."

Back in Action

In preparation for his fight with Mason, Rocky endured his most painful training yet. In the gym, Duke put him through a series of difficult maneuvers designed to increase his punching power. The punishing regime also finally allowed Rocky to let out some of the rage he had been feeling since Adrian's death.

Rocky built up his upper body strength with multiple repetitions.

To hone Rocky's reactions and balance all Duke needed was a basketball.

Punchy watches as Rocky lifts weights that would crush many younger men.

Thanks to Duke, Rocky is better shape than he has been for years.

Moments Away

Following the official weigh-in before the fight, Rocky approached the waiting Mason, with Robert by his side. Out of earshot from everyone else, Mason tried to lay down his own set of ground rules, emphasizing that there was no reason for anyone to get hurt. Mason expressed his willingness to do enough so that Rocky wouldn't have to be embarrassed, but, he warned, if Rocky attempted to "get it going," it would be something he would regret. When Rocky mentioned that losing wasn't part of his game plan, Mason seemed to find the notion amusing.

Pre-Fight

"SOME PEOPLE COME TO LAS VEGAS TO LOSE. I DIDN'T... AIN'T NOTHIN' OVER 'TIL IT'S OVER." Rocky

BEFORE ROCKY AND MASON walked away from each other at the weigh-in, Rocky asked whether or not Mason was even a little bit scared, but the champ confidently replied that nothing scared him. "That's good," Rocky confided to Robert when they were out of earshot, "You know, you try harder when you're scared." For the first time in many years, Robert allowed himself to feel proud of his remarkable father. Later in his hotel room, Rocky tried to stop his head spinning from all the crazy goings on. He was surprised but delighted when Marie showed up to wish him luck and give him some much-needed encouragement. She pointed out that if nothing else, the fight with Mason would prove that the last thing to age on somebody is their heart. Before she left, Marie handed Rocky a picture of Adrian that that he always kept in his van, adding, "She'll get you through this safe and sound."

The Arena

Rocky found himself transported back to a world he never thought he would be a part of again. He had missed boxing terribly over the past 15 years, but here he was being given one more shot to prove to himself—and to the rest of the world—that he could still go the distance.

Accompanied by Robert, Paulie, Duke, and even Spider-Rico, Rocky felt as though he had made peace with his past and was ready for the future.

The only thing missing from this moment of personal triumph was his beloved Adrian, but he knew that she would be there in spirit.

Already a Winner

Taking a moment before entering the arena, Rocky reflected that he was already grateful for everything this fight had brought him. He and Robert had connected for the first time in years, Paulie was still in his corner, and he had once again been driven by the inspirational words of Duke. More than that, his life was moving forward in a way that it hadn't since Adrian died: A new friendship had been discovered and quietly nurtured with Marie, and, aware of how differently his life could have gone, he had also gained respect for someone from his distant past—Spider-Rico. Win or lose the fight, Rocky was convinced he was far better off than he had been before Mason came calling.

Against the Odds

Rocky knew the odds—Mason had never even been knocked down before, but that just filled him with additional motivation. As he and Mason moved around the ring, Rocky was reminded of what Duke had told him about his first fight with Apollo. No one expected much of a fight, but Rocky proved everyone wrong. Tonight, just like 20 years earlier, Rocky got into the ring with the knowledge that he hadn't come for a show— he had come for a fight.

Rocky maintains his guard against Mason's punishing blows.

Mason realises that he should not underestimate Rocky.

Despite his injuries, Rocky is determined to go the distance.

The Last Fight

"LET THE BEAST OUT ONE LAST TIME"
PAULIE

WHEN THE FIGHT STARTED, Mason was true to his word. He set about putting on a good show for the public, while appearing to give Rocky due respect. He danced around the ring while skilfully avoiding Rocky's punches. He even delivered a few blows of his own here or there, but they weren't designed to cause his opponent any serious damage. But for Rocky, there was something very different at work. He had his own reasons for entering this fight and did not intend to play Mason's game. Not only did he need to prove his own ability, but he was suddenly engulfed with the realization that, at least for this moment, he needed to be there. It was a part of him and always had been. That self-knowledge gave him the courage to be there, and his skills as a fighter gave him the right. Now, despite the respect Rocky felt for him, Mason would be the focus for all the aging fighter's desire to prove that he could still go the distance. If Rocky could actually land a punch on the guy. And early on in the fight, that was a big "if."

A Real Fight

Early on, there was no denying that Mason was in full control of the fight, barely allowing Rocky to connect in any way. But then Rocky managed to gain a slight advantage and fought like the champion he used to be. Mason, was caught unaware, was engulfed in pain, but fought back. A ringside commentator who had been skeptical of Rocky earlier in the evening acknowledged, "There's an old saying, 'Beware of an aging great fighter—a great fighter may have one great fight left in him.' Well, folks, here it is tonight!"

As had been the intention from the beginning, each of Rocky's blows was like a pile-driver into Mason's head and body.

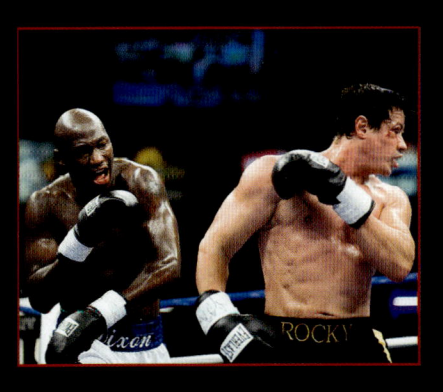

His life may have been a million to one shot, but Rocky Balboa always rose to the challenge.

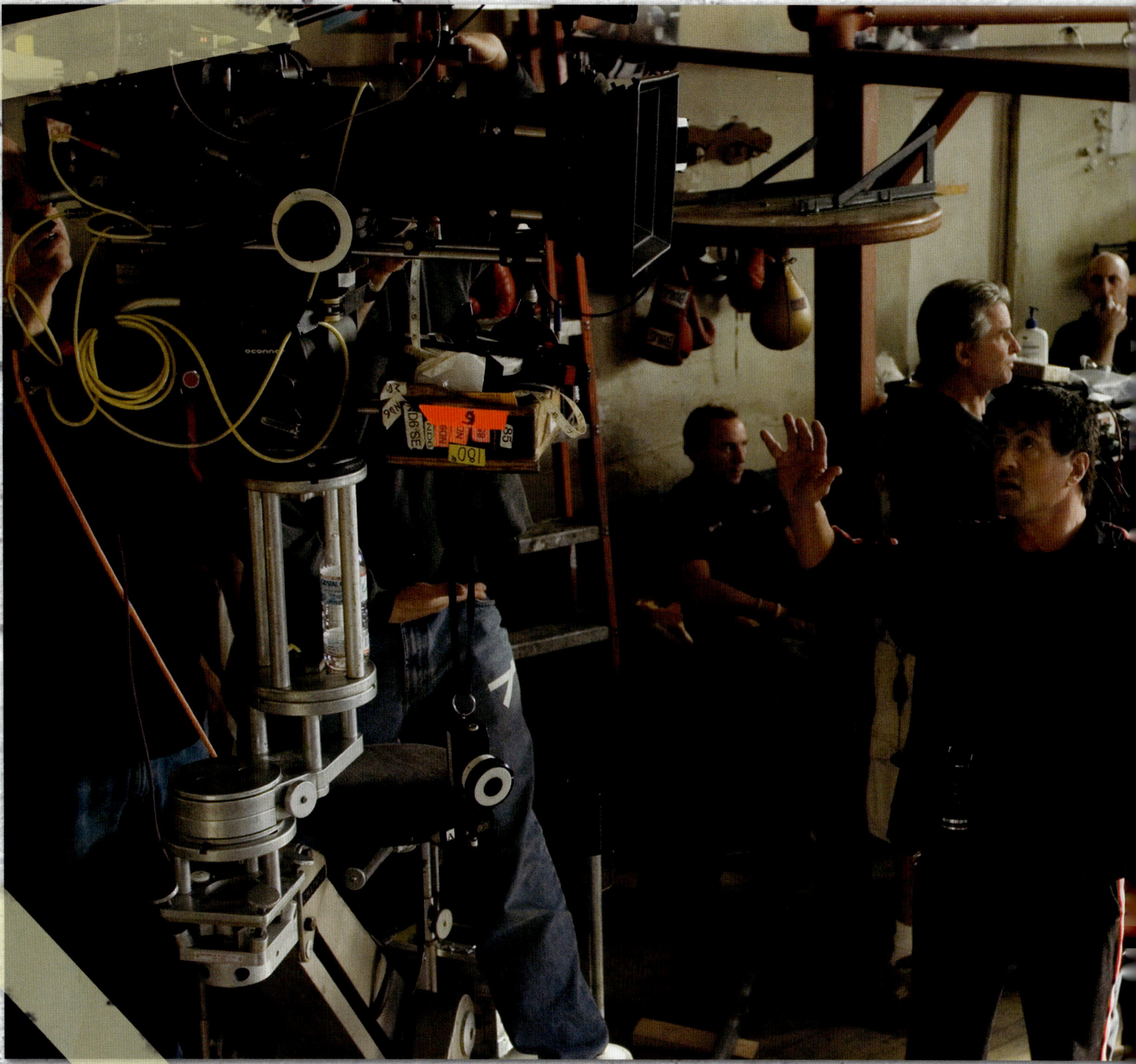

BEHIND THE SCENES

THIRTY YEARS AFTER he first stepped into the ring against Apollo Creed, Rocky Balboa remains one of the most unique and best-loved characters in movie history. Between the 1976 original *Rocky*, through the various sequels, to the release of the sixth film, *Rocky Balboa*, in 2006, generations of filmgoers have shared the different stages of the character's life, from his early years as a two-bit brawler, through to marriage, parenthood, success, failure, and success once again. Now, as an older and wiser Rocky Balboa prepares to enter the final stage of his life, we can take a closer look behind the scenes of this amazing movie franchise. For as fascinating as Rocky has been on screen, the making of his saga was in some ways just as eventful, as the following inside look at each film in the series reveals.

Rocky

THE HUMAN ELEMENT of *Rocky* was always going to be its biggest selling point, and it is certainly what attracted director John G. Avildsen to the movie. "A friend of mine sent the script to me and he had to convince me to read it, because I had no interest in boxing," Avildsen explains. "I thought it was a dumb sport. But he asked me to do him a favor and read it. And I had met Sylvester a couple of times before when he would come in an audition for different movies I was doing. So I read it, and on the second or third page this guy was talking to his turtles, Cuff and Link, and I was charmed. I found it to be a terrific character study with boxing as a background, just like the Civil War was the background of *Gone With the Wind*. I never figured this story was about boxing; it was about this guy who had a dream and I was very taken by it." Moviegoers the world over would be equally taken with the story, whether they were boxing fans or not.

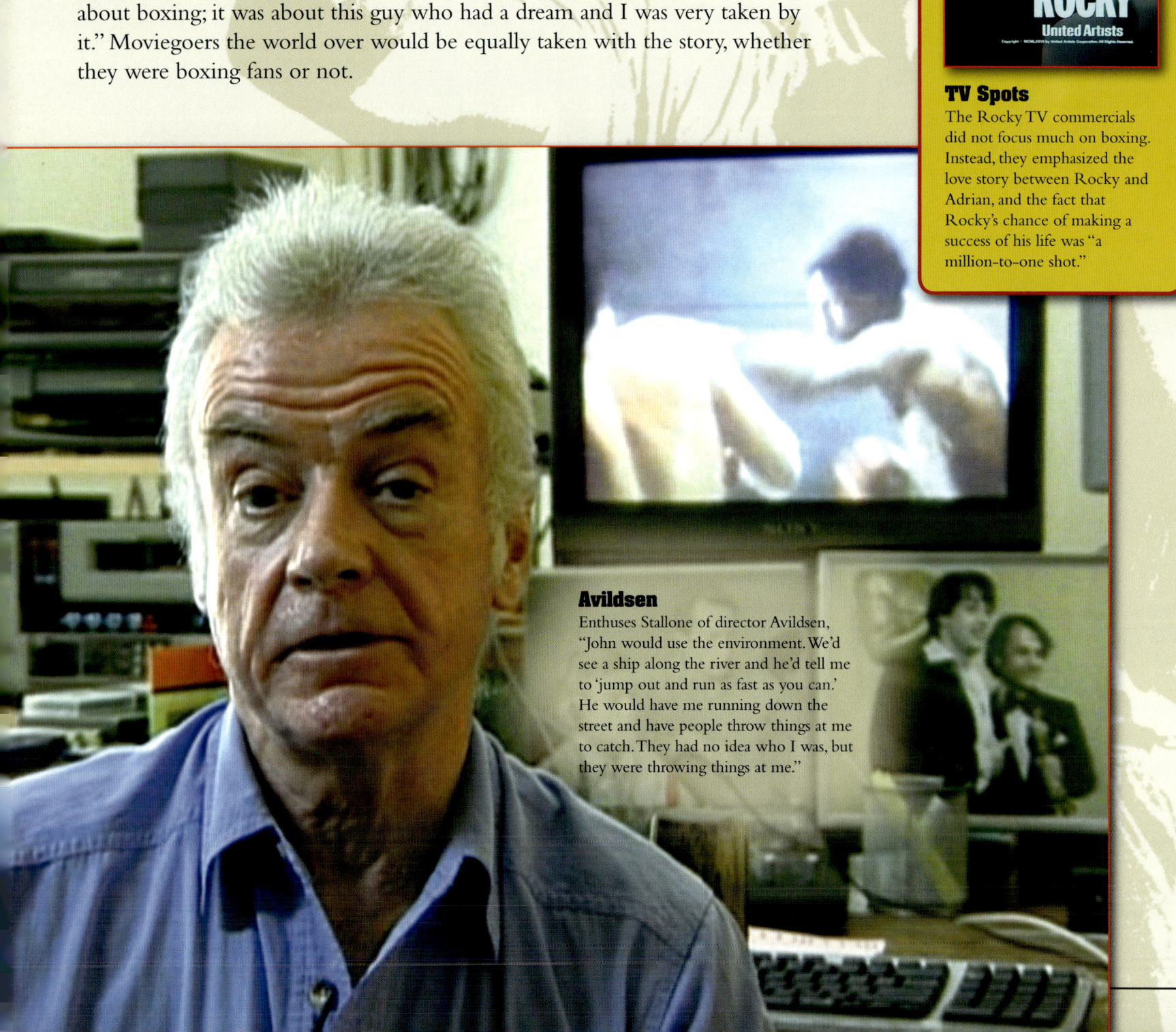

TV Spots
The Rocky TV commercials did not focus much on boxing. Instead, they emphasized the love story between Rocky and Adrian, and the fact that Rocky's chance of making a success of his life was "a million-to-one shot."

Avildsen
Enthuses Stallone of director Avildsen, "John would use the environment. We'd see a ship along the river and he'd tell me to 'jump out and run as fast as you can.' He would have me running down the street and have people throw things at me to catch. They had no idea who I was, but they were throwing things at me."

Steadicam

Garrett Brown's Steadicam, which would revolutionize filmmaking by removing the shakiness of hand-held cameras, was used for the first time in *Rocky*. In an *American Cinematographer* profile of Brown, the magazine noted, "The most famous scene in the original *Rocky* shot by Brown is also Stallone's most famous moment on film—Rocky's run up the steps of the Philadelphia Museum of Art…The Steadicam was also used extensively in the fight scenes… Never before were audiences taken into the fray by a camera, never before had action scenes appeared so realistically as they did in this movie."

Fight Rehearsals

Recalling how the fight sequences in *Rocky* were choreographed, Avildsen reflects, "I said to Sylvester, 'Why don't you go home and write this thing out: left, right, up, down…whatever you want, and then we'll learn that like a ballet?' The next day Sylvester came back with thirty-some pages of lefts and rights. I had my 8mm movie camera and started shooting them do it. I'd show them the footage every day and they'd see how terrible it looked, and came up with ways to make it better and we got it down."

KEEPING IT IN THE FAMILY

It was not just out of loyalty that Stallone brought family members into the *Rocky* cast. In truth, with the film being produced on such a low budget, it was necessary for Stallone to call in favors from friends and family to save money.

Father Figure

Stallone's father was cast in the role of bell ringer—a role which which reportedly ended up in a family feud when he forgot to ring the bell as his son was being pummeled by Carl Weathers.

Man's Best Friend

It was decided that Rocky should have a dog who could go running with him when he trained. When asked if he had a pet they could use, Stallone replied, "I have a thing called Butkus that's a throwback to the Stone Age."

Brotherly Love

Stallone's brother Frank was brought on board in *Rocky* as the leader of a group of guys standing around a burning garbage can and singing different songs a capella. In *Rocky II*, Rocky was to tell Adrian that the guys were the "neighborhood jukebox."

133

Rocky II, III, IV, & V

UNLESS YOUR NAME was Michel Corleone or James Bond, back in the 1970s Hollywood looked down upon sequels. But after *Rocky* won the Academy Award for Best Picture of the Year, Sylvester Stallone started to change all of that. He began to see Rocky as an opportunity to do something a little different. "If you have a character that's well liked and if you can use the character in a successful film that has a message applicable to today, why desert him?" Stallone argued. "I've never understood that, which is why I don't like any of my characters to die. Killing them off is just too Hemingwayesque for me. I don't need to have any matador at the end of a bull's horn and being paraded through the streets of Pamplona. I'd much rather have him jump on the bull's back and ride into the sunset, and maybe we'll see where he goes in the future."

This poster was created in the style of old-time boxing posters.

Rocky II

When the original *Rocky* captured the imagination of the world and the small $1 million movie went on to gross an astounding $100 million globally, there seemed no question that there would be a follow-up. The challenge was ensuring that the sequel existed for a legitimate reason—that its story would be a natural progression from the events of the original film and not just an attempt to stretch the idea as far as it would go. "With *Rocky II*," said Sylvester Stallone, "the question was, 'Do we go for quality or just for money?' The whole team agreed that we'd walk away before we would grind out a potboiler to capitalize on *Rocky*. I like Rocky. To me, he's a 20th century gladiator in a pair of sneakers and a hat, and he's out of sync with the times. When I first thought about doing *Rocky II*, I wanted to have him fight in the Coliseum in Rome. I think about giving him more glamour, but that also meant giving up the neighborhood, the street corner, the guys back in Philadelphia. If he were to become Continental and big-time, I think I'd lose the essence of Rocky. Rather than make it big, his world should remain within a three-block radius in Philadelphia." Thus it was decided that the focus in *Rocky II* would remain on the ensemble of characters introduced in the first film, Rocky's marriage to Adrian and, of course, his rematch with Apollo Creed.

Carl Weathers reprised his role as Apollo Creed.

This one-sheet design was one of the most iconic of the 1980s.

Rocky III

When the time came to return to the boxing ring for a third installment, Sylvester Stallone was determined to make the new film different from its predecessors. "With *Rocky III*, I wanted to reveal the flip side of the fame game. We're conditioned to cope with failure, but there are no platitudes for dealing with success. Seven years had passed since *Rocky*. Panic and fear set in. I used those emotions to get back to the person I was before all the glamour and notoriety. Rocky is a once-in-a-lifetime coming together of self and character. I think there's an interesting story in what happens to a man after he has been on top. Could he do it again if he had to? Has Rocky peaked? Is he softer, less daring? What does he do when he recognizes that a younger fighter has come along who could be the very one to take his title away?" With these questions in mind, Stallone portrayed Rocky as a man who had lost his hunger and then his title and goes back to his roots to regain it all.

Mr. T as Clubber Lang was the opponent that fans loved to hate.

Sylvester Stallone contemplates a shot on the set of Rocky III, *which would beat its predecessors at the box office.*

134

Rocky IV

Boxing enters the Cold War as Rocky takes on Soviet champion Ivan Drago (Dolph Lundgren) following the death of Apollo Creed at the Russian's hands. Of this particular battle, Sylvester Stallone offers, "Drago has always seen himself as invincible. He represents technology, big business, machines, international politics. His fighting is mechanical; Rocky is a street fighter. Finally, Drago sees the system that created him for what it is and he turns on it. But neither side walks away clean. The fighters come out and try to destroy, maim, and kill each other and both are damaged. There are no victors in boxing. Rocky learns it all comes down to change, compromise. That's the name of the game." Amusingly, Stallone was juggling *Rocky IV* and *Rambo: First Blood Part II* at about the same time. "There were times I wasn't quite sure whether I should be picking up a machine gun or putting on my boxing gloves," he laughed.

Rocky IV became the second highest-grossing movie of 1985.

Before they became actors, Carl Weathers had been a professional football player and Dolph Lundgren a karate champion.

Playing brother Paulie and sister Adrian in the Rocky movies, Burt Young and Talia Shire were also good friends in real life.

Rocky V

Rocky V starred real-life boxer Tommy Morrison as Rocky's young protégé. Morrison, the great nephew of legendary actor John Wayne, briefly became WBO Heavyweight Champion of the World in 1993. The movie brought the Italian Stallion full-circle—from down on his luck boxer, to champion and millionaire, and, back again—to the streets where it all started. "Rocky," Stallone explained, "becomes the guiding force behind a younger man [Tommy Morrison's Tommy Gunn]. He teaches him with all his heart, and this man turns out to be everything he detests in the world. I'm trying to say if you create a bad situation, it is your responsibility to cleanse it, to purge it and not depend on anyone else. [Meanwhile], Rocky's boy is trying to pull him into the past by the mere fact that he's a young Rocky. But Rocky can't go back. Mickey's dead. Apollo's dead, and a piece of his life is dead—but he's just driven by it. When you start trying to go backwards, though, that's what kills you. So many of these old boxers, they're crazed, they're absolutely nuts; you see a lot of them in prison or on drugs or being sparring partners just to get a taste of it. Because what else do they have?"

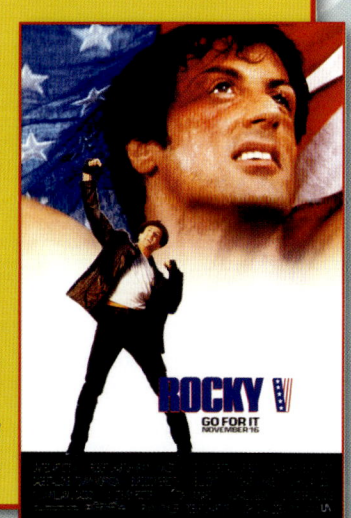

Stallone believes that Talia Shire's Adrian is the heart and soul of the Rocky films.

Rocky Jr. was played by Sylvester Stallone's real-life son, Sage.

For years fans believed this would be their final image of Rocky.

Rocky Balboa

CRAFTING THE FIRST Rocky film in 15 years presented everyone involved with a host of new challenges, despite the vast amount of experience they had garnered from the earlier moves. For Sylvester Stallone, it's all about coming to grips with the notion of getting older, exploring the meaning of doing so, and demanding that society not discount a person simply because, as Rocky puts it in the film, "you've celebrated too many birthdays." Says the actor/writer/director of the film, "They say he's too old. Well, of course he's older and well past his prime. But he's drawn back into the ring as a sort of publicity stunt, and out of what starts off as a joke, he pulls it off. I have written it to show people life isn't over at 40 or 50. People want to move you out of the way, but I say you walk around me. Age is this insidious weasel that creeps up on you out of nowhere, but I'm still in my prime."

Production

Although Sylvester Stallone and Antonio Tarver were earlier filmed in a virtual ring for the computer generated fight, actual production on the budget-conscious 38-day shoot began in December 2005 at Las Vegas' Mandalay Bay Resort & Casino. After shooting the boxing match there, the production moved in January to Rocky's hometown of Philadelphia, Pennsylvania for the majority of filming, before a final move to Los Angeles, California.

A New Opponent

In former light heavyweight champion Antonio Tarver, Stallone knew he had found the perfect man to play Mason "The Line" Dixon. Says Tarver, "Sylvester Stallone believes in this movie, and he wants the best. We've been working a lot of long hours and I think the people are going to be surprised at how real this is. People won't know the difference between a fight with me and Roy Jones Jr. and a fight with me and Rocky Balboa. This is what's going to sell this movie."

Since the original Rocky *30 years ago, Stallone has insisted the boxing matches have a sense of realism.*

Tarver, Stallone, and Mike Tyson look like they're ready to take on the world—or each other.

Tommy Morrison is Rocky V, and Antonio Tarver are the only real-life boxers to fight Rocky.

Stallone had the concept for Rocky Balboa *years ago, but needed to convince studios the time was right.*

Fight choreography: treating the fight like a dance routine was an integral part to pulling the bout off.

Dressed in Rocky's exterior work-out gear, Sylvester Stallone decides on just the right shot.

Stallone, dressed in full Rocky street regalia, stands incongruously behind the camera.

As writer, director, and star Sylvester Stallone has to look at the movie from different angles.

Under a very limited time schedule, crew members work as hard as they can to pull different elements together.

Stallone, accompanied by a Steadicam prepares for a shot that will bring the audience into Rocky's world.

Back where it began 30 years earlier, Sylvester Stallone is ready for action on the streets of Philadelphia.

This time when he climbs the steps leading to the art musuem, Rocky is accompanied by his mutt, Punchy.

Behind the Scenes: Props

Rocky's Hat
When audiences were first introduced to Rocky Balboa, he had the look of a hood, adorned in leather jacket and this hat. It was appropriate attire for Tony Gazzo's enforcer, but not for a champion, and Rocky discarded the look as success came his way. Interestingly, when the character lost his money in *Rocky V* and was returned to his roots, Sylvester Stallone elected to bring the hat out of retirement.

Gloves
In Ancient Greece, Olympic boxers wore only leather straps on their hands and wrists for protection. The first padded gloves, known as "mufflers," were invented by English heavyweight champ Jack Broughton in 1743. Later, in 1867, more modern-looking gloves, described as resembling a bloated pair of mittens, were introduced. These evolved into the kind of gloves worn by Rocky—a style which has changed little to the present day.

Padded gloves reduce the risk serious injury.

Civilized
In this sequence from *Rocky III*, Rocky has gotten into the ring with Clubber Lang for a rematch in which he retakes the title from him. As a fight, it's a wonder to behold, but it was far more civilized than what fans of the sport experienced in Ancient Rome. In those days, fighters were usually criminals or slaves, who would battle each other in the hope of becoming a champion and thereby gaining their freedom. Boxing apparently became so popular that many free people wanted to participate as well. It was eventually banned as a sport in 500 B.C. by Theodoric the Great.

Everyone has a favorite fight from the Rocky films, but this remains one of the most exciting.

Corporation sponsorship in the Rocky films!

A full view of Rocky's boxing footwear.

The name of Paulie's employer.

Rocky's self-given nickname.

Rocky prepares to enter the arena a walking billboard.

"Paulie gets three grand, I get the robe."

The Robe
Rocky's baggy satin robe, emblazoned with the name of the meat plant Paulie worked at, became the brunt of several jokes not only in the original *Rocky*, but *Rocky II* as well. Desperate to cash in on Rocky's success, Paulie worked out a deal with his boss that he would be paid $3,000 if the large "Shamrock Meats, Inc." was displayed across the back of the robe. Needless to say, the sign didn't appear on robes Rocky wore for his later appearances, after he had achieved fame.

These trunks have been through wars!

If Trunks Could Talk....
What a legacy: Apollo wore these stars and stripes trunks in his first fight with Rocky, then offered them to him for his rematch with Clubber Lang. The trunks made their way back to Apollo for his battle to the death with Drago, and Rocky reacquired them for his own fight with the Russian. Then they were loaned to Tommy Gunn, who won the heavyweight championship wearing them.

Glossary

Drago lands a left hook on Apollo

B

BLOCKING – The use of hands, arms, or shoulders to prevent an opponent landing a punch.
BOB – A defensive move where the head is moved below and to the side of an opponent's punch.
BOOTS – Footwear worn by the boxer which support their feet and ankles.
BOUT – A match between two boxers, with a minimum of four, and a maximum of twelve, three-minute rounds with a one minute break between each round.
BREAK – An order from the referee for the two boxers to separate from a clinch. When "break" is called, both boxers must take a step back.

C

CAUTION – A referee's remonstration to a boxer, for a minor rule infringement.
CLINCH – Also known as "holding", this is when two boxers lean on each other, without throwing punches.
COACH – The person who trains a boxer and gives them ringside advice and encouragement.
COMBINATION – A sequence of different types of punches.
CORNER – Either of the two corners of the ring assigned to each boxer and their team.
COUNTERPUNCH – A punch thrown as a counterattack to an opponent's lead.
COVERING – A method of defense where the hands are held in front of the face, and the arms against the torso.
CROSS – A shoulder level punch usually made with the dominant fist, crossing over the leading hand.
CUT MAN – The person who administers to the boxers' cuts and swelling between rounds.

F

FEINT – A deceptive move where the boxer fakes a punch to put their opponent into a vulnerable position. This can be both an offensive and defensive tactic.
FLYWEIGHT – A division of boxers' weight of not more than 112 lb (51kg).
FOOTWORK – The way a boxer manouevers their feet to fight as effectively as possible.
FOUL – A violation of boxing rules.

G

GLOVES – Boxers wear these on their hands to prevent breaks and bruising.

H

HAND WRAPS – Bandages worn under the gloves used to protect the bones in the hand and prevent them from breaking.
HEADGEAR – Protective padding against swelling and cuts. This is not permitted in professional boxing, but must be worn in amateur boxing.

Rocky and Drago in a bout

HEAVYWEIGHT – A division of boxers' weight of more than 79kg/175 lb.
HOOK – A short, power punch using the back and shoulder muscles with the arm usually bent at a 90 degree angle, which brings the fist from the side to the centre. It is normally aimed at the head or liver.

J

JAB – A fast, straight, arm-length punch thrown with the leading hand.
JUDGE – One of the three officials who scores a boxing match.

K

KNOCK-DOWN – When a boxer touches the floor with any part of the body other than their feet, go outside the ropes, or take a significant blow or blows to the head (even if they have not fallen down).
KNOCK-OUT – Declared by the referee if a boxer has been floored longer than a count of ten.

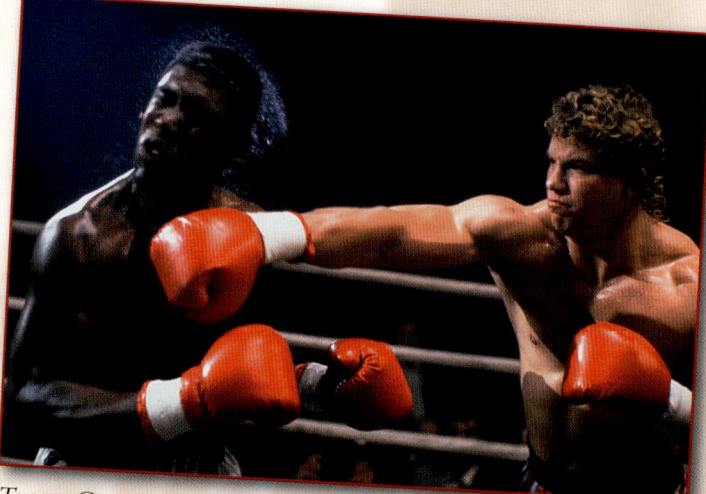

Tommy Gunn throws a powerful right jab.

L

LIGHTWEIGHT – A division of boxers' weight of 126-132 lb. (59-61 kg).
LOW BLOW – Any punch that lands

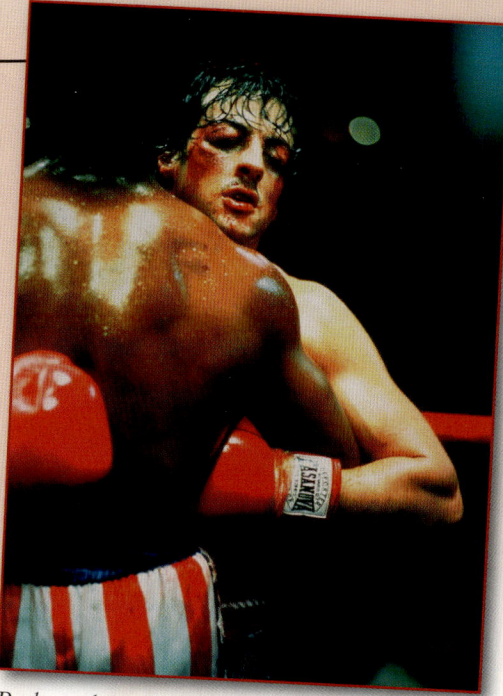

Rocky and Apollo are held in a clinch.

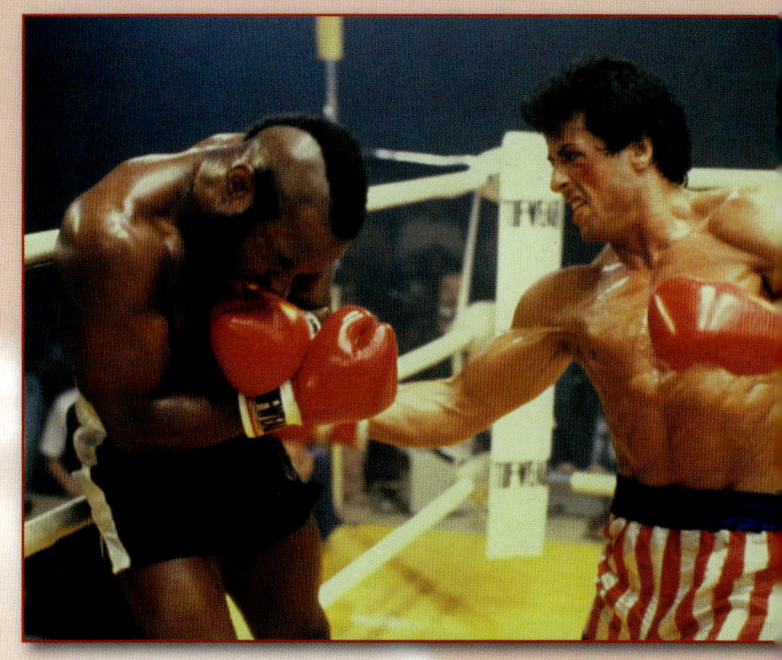

Rocky delivers an uppercut into Clubber Lang's chin

below the top of the opponent's hips.

M

MAJORITY DECISION – When two of the three judges agree upon the winner of a bout, and the third has scored it as a draw.
MANAGER – The person who runs the business career of a boxer.
MIDDLEWEIGHT – A division of boxers' weight of 157-465 lb (70-72.5kg).
MOUTHPIECE – A piece of plastic worn by a boxer to protect their teeth and prevent them biting their tongue. Also known as a "Gumshield".

N

NEUTRAL CORNERS – The two corners not used by either boxer.
NO DECISION – When the judges declare that there is no winner after a match.

P

POINT – The system used to score a bout. Two out of the three judges must be in agreement for a boxer to be awarded a point. If there is no knock-out then the winner of a bout is decided upon points.

R

RABBIT PUNCH – An illegal punch to the base of the skull, the neck or body (usually the kidney area).

REFEREE – The offficial who stands within the ring to enforce rules and ensure that a match is fair.
RING – The square space in which boxers fight.
RINGSIDE PHYSICIAN – The doctor who ensures that boxers are in good condition, and who decides whether a boxer is well enough to continue fighting. They hold the authority to halt a match.
ROUND – One of a series of fights, divided by breaks, which make up a boxing match (bout).

S

SECOND – A person other than the coach who lends the boxer advice and encouragement ringside.
SLIP (or SLIPPING) – A defensive move where the boxer quickly rotates their hips and shoulders, without moving their feet backward. Their chin moves sideways so an oncoming punch passes them by.
SPARRING – Practise fights between boxers, an important part of training.
SPLIT DECISION – When two of the three judges decide that one boxer is the winner of a bout, but the third jusdge has scored the opponent as such.
STANCE – The way a boxer places their feet and holds their body in order to best deliver punches.

T

THROWING IN THE TOWEL – A signal to the referee that a boxer wishes to retire from a match, usually given by a boxer's second.

U

UPPERCUT – A power punch using the rear fist, starting from the belly and thrown upwards to strike from beneath, usually on the chin.

W

WARNING – The referee issues this to a boxer who has already received three cautions and the judges can subsequently decide whether to award the opponent a point. A boxer is disqualified if they are given three warnings in a bout.
WELTERWEIGHT – A division of boxers' weight of 140-147 lb (63.5-66.5 kg).
WEAVE – Turning and twisting motions made by a boxer to evade a punch.
WRIST WRAPS – Bandages worn under gloves used to protect the wrist-bones and prevent breakages.

Rocky wears protective headgear to avoid cuts and swelling.

Index

A

Academy Awards 9, 11
accountant 96, 98, 114
Adrian 14, 16-17, 20, 21, 29, 33, 34, 35, 36, 37, 38, 39, 40, 48, 55, 59, 61, 68, 69, 79, 83, 92, 96, 97, 98, 101, 103, 104, 105, 109, 110, 114, 116, 117, 125, 135
Ali, Muhammad 8
American Bicentennial 11, 18, 26
Art Museum, Philadelphia 24, 41, 82, 103, 111, 133, 137
auction 97
Avildsen, John G. 9, 91, 132, 133

B

bell 43, 62, 86, 109
brain damage 91, 96, 122
Brown, Garrett 133
Brown, James 74
Butkus 17, 133

C

cameraman 109
Cane, Union 93, 106, 107
Carmine, Father 33, 103
Chartoff, Robert 8, 9
chaperones 82
choreography 131, 135
Cold War 67

coma 38, 39
Commission 122
confidence 60, 61
Conti, Bill 9
Creed, Apollo 18-19, 20, 21, 24, 26, 27, 28, 29, 31, 32, 34, 36, 39, 41, 42, 43, 44, 45, 48, 56, 59, 60, 61, 62, 63, 65, 68, 69, 72, 73, 74, 75, 76, 77, 78, 79, 82, 84, 86, 87, 98, 102, 106, 115, 131, 135
Cuff and Link 115, 132
cufflink 98, 102

D

Dixon, Mason "The Line" 118-119, 120, 121, 122, 123, 125, 126, 127, 128, 129, 136, 137
Drago, Ivan 67, 68, 69, 70-71, 72, 73, 75, 76, 77, 78, 79, 80, 81, 82, 83, 85, 86, 87, 88, 89, 91, 92, 93, 94, 96, 109, 110, 135, 139
Drago, Ludmilla 70, 71, 72, 75, 81, 88
drugs 71 81
Duke, Tony (Apollo's trainer) 26, 36, 42, 43, 45, 77, 80, 82, 83, 92, 122, 125, 127
Duke, George Washington 93, 94-95, 99, 102, 103, 106, 107, 108, 109, 110

E

Eye of the tiger 18, 59, 61
"Eye of the Tiger" 47

F

family 104, 105, 111, 114, 131
father, Rocky's 12, 22
favor 63, 64-65
Frazier, Joe 137
funeral
  of Mickey 59
  of Apollo Creed 78

G

Gazzo, Tony 12, 13, 14, 17, 22, 33, 35, 138
gloves 138
Goldmill, Mickey *see* Mickey
Gunn, Tommy 99, 100-101, 102, 103, 104, 105, 106, 107, 108, 109, 114, 117, 135, 139

H

hat 98, 138
heavyweight 18, 23, 24, 28, 33, 63, 103, 106-7, 115, 118, 133
"home team" 97, 104

I

Itallian Stallion, the 11, 12-13, 19, 20, 26, 31, 34, 40, 47, 81, 88

J

Jergens, George 20, 21

K

Koloff, Nikoli 71, 72, 79

L

Lang, Clubber 47, 49, 52–53, 54, 55, 56, 57, 59, 60, 61, 62, 63, 64, 65, 67, 68, 69, 83, 138, 139, 132
Las Vegas 74, 118, 136
Lee Green, Mac 18, 19
Lil Marie *see* Marie
Lundgren, Dolph 135

M

Marciano, Rocky 12, 24, 98
Morrison, Tommy 133
Marie 116, 124, 127
Martin 118, 119
Meredith, Burgess 9
Meat Packers, Shamrock 14, 24, 114, 139
Mickey 9, 22-23, 24, 25, 33, 35, 36, 37, 38, 40, 42, 45, 48, 51, 53, 55, 56, 59, 84, 92, 98, 99, 109
motorcycles 97
Muppet Show, the 48

P

Paulie 14-15, 17, 20, 24, 33, 35, 37, 59, 68, 80, 82, 85, 92, 93, 96, 98, 101, 103, 104, 107, 108, 114, 116, 117, 122, 125, 127, 129, 135, 139
Pennino, Paulie *see* Paulie
Philadelphia Spectrum 21, 26
pilgrimage 114
prayer 38, 39, 84
Punchy 117, 125, 137
puppet 100, 102

R

Rambo: First Blood Part II 133
realism 135
rehearsals 131
re-license 122
revenge 86
right-handed 40
robe 14, 139
Robert 96, 97, 98, 104, 105, 109, 111, 114, 116, 117, 120, 125, 126, 127
Rocky Jr. 39, 68, 135
 also see Robert
Rocky's 115
Russia 67, 69, 70, 71, 80, 81, 86, 96, 106
Russian(s) 69, 71, 73, 76, 78, 79, 81, 86, 88, 139

S

shool 104
Shire, Talia 9, 135
skating rink 9, 17
Southpaw 18, 26, 40, 42, 45
Soviet Union 68, 88
Spider-Rico 12, 13, 115, 116, 127
Stallone, Frank 133
Stallone, Sage 135
Stallion Chicken, the 36, 37
statue 54, 59
Steadicam 8, 133, 137
Steps 116, 117
Stevenson *see* Steps

T

T., Mr. 47, 134
Tarver, Antonio 136, 137
Taxes 97
Thunderlips 50-51
trainer 99, 118
training 24-25, 40-41, 56, 80, 81, 102-103, 124-125
trunks 27, 74, 102, 139
turtles 17, 130

V

Vietnam War 11
virtual reality contest 120, 121

W

Watergate 11
Weathers, Carl 9, 133, 134, 135
Wedding 33
Wepner, Chuck 8
Winkler, Robert 8

Y

Young, Burt 135

DK

LONDON, NEW YORK
MELBOURNE, MUNICH AND DELHI

SENIOR EDITOR Catherine Saunders
PROJECT EDITOR Julia March
EDITORIAL ASSISTANT Elizabeth Noble
PUBLISHING MANAGER Simon Beecroft
SENIOR DESIGNER Nathan Martin
BRAND MANAGER Robert Perry
DTP DESIGNER Hanna Ländin
CATEGORY PUBLISHER Alex Allan
PRODUCTION CONTROLLER Rochelle Talary

First Published in Great Britain in 2007 by
Dorling Kindersley Limited,
80 Strand, London, WC2R 0RL

Copyright © 2007 Dorling Kindersley Limited
A Penguin Company

2 4 6 8 10 9 7 5 3 1
RD136 – 11/06

Rocky, Rocky II, Rocky III, Rocky IV, and Rocky V ™ & © 1976-2007 Metro-Goldwyn-Mayer Studios, Inc.
All Rights Reserved.
ROCKY BALBOA © 2007 Metro-Goldwyn-Mayer Pictures Inc., Colombia Pictures Industries, Inc. and Revolution
Studios Distribution Company, LLC.
ROCKY BALBOA is a trademark of Metro-Goldwyn-Meyer Studios Inc. All Rights Reserved.

All rights reserved. No part of this publication may be reproduced, stored in a retrieval system, or transmitted in any
form or by any means, electronic, mechanical, photocopying, recording, or otherwise, without the prior written
permission of the copyright owner.

A CIP catalogue record for this book is available from the British Library.

ISBN: 978-1-40532-001-6

Colour reproduction by Media Development and Printing, UK.
Printed and bound in China by Leo Paper Products, Ltd.

MGM would like to thank the following people: Kevin King, Celeste Salzer, and Ralph Brescia for their time and
insight; Nathan, Catherine, and Rob for their talent and vision, and especially Alex at DK who was willing to say
"yes" when all around her said "no"; Edward Gross, for his wealth of knowledge; and the gentleman without whom
this book wouldn't be possible, Sylvester Stallone—Thank you.

The author would like to dedicate this book to his wife and best friend, Eileen.

The Publishers have made every effort to secure permissions for use of all likenesses in the book.

**Discover more at
www.dk.com**